Relics of Lust

New and Selected Poems

Also by Lynne Savitt

Lust in 28 Flavors, Second Coming Press, 1979

Eros Unbound, Blue Horse Publications, 1980

No Apologies, Cardinal Press, 1981

Plump Passions, Ancient Mariners Press, 1988

Dreams As Erect As Nipples on Ice, Ghost Dance, 1989

Sleeping Retrospect of Desire, Konocti Books, 1993

The Burial of Longing Beneath the Blue Neon Moon, Ye Olde Font Shoppe, 1999

The Transport of Grandma's Yearning Vibrator, Myshkin Press, 2002

Greatest Hits 1979–2003, Pudding House Publications, 2004

The Deployment of Love in Pineapple Twilight, Presa Press, 2005

Digging Dinosaur Dignity in Ardortown, Myshkin Press, 2008

Too Late for Valentine's Day, Myshkin Press, 2012

Relics of Lust

New and Selected Poems

Lynne Savitt

NŊY Books™

The New York Quarterly Foundation, Inc.
New York, New York

NYQ Books™ is an imprint of The New York Quarterly Foundation, Inc.

The New York Quarterly Foundation, Inc.
P. O. Box 2015
Old Chelsea Station
New York, NY 10113

www.nyq.org

First Edition

Set in New Baskerville

Layout and Design by Raymond P. Hammond
Cover photo by Noelle Crough
Author photos by George William Fisher
Brown bottle image: ©iStockphoto.com/AM-C
Green bottle image: ©iStockphoto.com/bluestocking

Library of Congress Control Number: 2014931066

ISBN: 978-1-935520-82-5

Relics of Lust

New and Selected Poems

Acknowledgments

The New York Quarterly, 13th Moon, 24-7, Alpha Beat Soup, Anthills, Axe Factory, A Good Day to Die, Atom Mind, Banshee, Bartleby's Review, Bouillabaisse, The Butcher's Block, Caprice, Cerberus, The Chiron Review, Coldspring Journal, Connections, December, Desolation Angels, Diana's Bimonthly, Ecstatic Peace, Gravida, Hollow Spring Review, Home Planet News, Hyperion, Imprint, Lummox, The Louisiana Review, Masquerade, Nitty Gritty, Occasional Review, One Trick Pony, Opinion Rag, Painted Bride Quarterly, Once More with Feeling, Pearl, Pig Iron, Poets, Poets-On-Line, Poetry Now, Presa, Red Cedar Review, Riverrat Review, Purple, Quick Brown Fox, Rattle, Red Cedar Review, Redstart, Rusty Truck, Sipapu, Scree, Second Coming, Stonecloud, Swamproot, Thunder Sandwich, Voices on the Vine, Womanchild, Yellow Brick Road, ZZZ ZYNE.

Anthologies: *A New Geography of Poets, Between the Cracks, Inside the Outside: An Anthology of Avant-Garde American Poets, Which Lillith?*

Special thanks to the swizzle sticks who've stirred the liquid of my desire for decades, GWF & OB.

for Allyson & Matthew,
my eternal éclairs of love

Contents

DREAMS AS ERECT AS NIPPLES ON ICE

LUST IN 28 FLAVORS

1979

ON BEING ASKED FOR BIOGRAPHICAL INFORMATION

i am terrified of biographies,
the factual black and white
printed credibility

the date the cloud was filled with lemon snowflakes

the hour my father exploded my birth from a tennis ball

the job at the orphanage giving oatmeal
kisses to homeless midwest cheeks

thumbprints from my offspring, my husband's
picture of my sister looking just like daddy
distributing dollars with a miser's heart
xerox copies of my mother's bridal dinner,
hysterectomy, charity luncheon
list of the religious persuasions and vegetable
preferences of all my lovers

there are new methods to categorize
fears, health habits, insecurities
all recorded on asbestos uniforms
worn by airline stewards on international flights

"born in australia in the emerald-studded
pouch of a sable-coated kangaroo
my right eye is a perfect star sapphire"

i am in favor of myths.

MY DADDY HAD A SEXTANT

I reached for the belt of Orion
        and looked for his fly
Stuck my hand in to find such
        vast black emptiness
Where are those thousand bursts
        of hot sparklers
That gush and spurt their energy
        clear to earth?

My sky seems barren and even the
        constellations
Leave me lonely as they shine
        only for the navigator

I could not illuminate the navigator's
        life
He was not moonstruck
        He saw ONLY the stars

Daddy did not want lunar light
        to love or fly in
All he ever wanted was a sun.

I'M GLAD YOU ARE CASUALLY INTERESTED IN WHY I WAS AN HOUR LATE/ OR TAKE YOUR FUCKING HANDS OFF MY THROAT

You were right my mountain of morality
                        I have to admit
I was in Port Authority
                        twirling tasseled tits
For an audience of hundreds that
                        happened to include
Four Hells Angels
Two Black Panthers
Seven bums that were stewed.

                        I did my show
                                leopard G-string on
                        And when my audience
                                was almost gone
                        My leather-clad phantom
                                took me away
                        On his beautiful Lightning BSA
                        He was an expert
                                knew what to do
                        We won a Silver Cup
                                in the power shift screw

He beat me up
                and threw me out
Then I deflowered two priests
                and three Boy Scouts
                        The cigarettes you found in
                                the backseat
                        Belong to three sailors
                                I happened to eat
                        Don't tell me, Darling,
                                that it's crude
                        You know I just adore seafood!

Isn't it amazing
       my energetic power?
I did those things
       in just one hour?

              You'd like to believe it
                 my adorable mate
              Not that I dropped Chuck at the
subway
                and class let out late
This is a love poem
       of sorts, my dear.
Because I am telling you
       what you wanted to hear.

THE MECHANICS OF LOVE

i am taking the brush to bed.

he is my father.

you do not understand
the mechanics of love.

i need to be shared.

how we accomplish this
is under discussion.

you may have my right
shoulder and inner thighs

for which you have
shown a preference.

my tongue is spoken
for and my cunt the

first to go you
will not mind it
not being your favorite part.

the rest is up for grabs
painfully enough to go around

and enough to convince you
of my earnest belief in punishment

in the yielding of my father
upon my most vulnerable parts.

if you cannot master the brush
leave my bed my love chamber

watching the welts rise
by themselves before you go.

IT'S HARD TO BE PROUD OF BEING JEWISH WHEN YOUR ONLY RELIGIOUS EXPERIENCE WAS SEEING *EXODUS*

We had been religious
under the aqua comforter with chartreuse
grasshoppers Saturday night
You went home
fingering your rosaries

When you surprised me
at ten Sunday morning
I was eating a bagel
You screamed, "I smell lox!"
I was caught

You forgot I make great lasagna
This perfect nose is my own
And, oh, those uncircumcised nights!

You, not afraid of the dark,
proctoscope, bad
movies or impotence
You, afraid of my family tree

We will picnic near *your* roots.

ON THE HOSPITALIZATION OF MY DAUGHTER FOR DIABETES

all my plans
                    we cannot run
                              away now
all my plans
                    for covering our nipples
                                   with forest leaves
                    digging our toes into plush cream
                    carpet of a san francisco apartment
                    hiding out with donald duck for weeks
                                   at disneyland
no one was going to be able to find us my green
                                   eyed daughter
grandma, brother, your long gone father would
search the editorial offices, bookshops, readings
& we'd be in oregon, arizona, montana, idaho
& we'd be tying flowers, shells on a string
                                   in our hair
all my plans
                    for kissing the suntanned knees
                    of old california lovers
the knuckles of beer breath loggers
you
     the perfect daughter
you
     the perfect star
you
     the perfect
all my plans
                    for the nuclear holocaust
                    survival of the strongest
and you will need your insulin
all my nightmares
                    a newly knit muffler
                                   choking my summer spirit

i fill the syringe
i rub your perfect thigh with alcohol
oh, my perfect
oh, my plans
oh, my daughter...

ELLEN'S BROTHER

Ellen had three snot-nosed kids
a house, a husband gone four years
Her brother came
to help when no man was around
He'd tune up the old car
take down the storm windows
carry in cases of beer
treat the kids at McDonald's

One night he came to our house
down the block to see if
I could help him with his
freshman lit paper
(you were at a faculty meeting)
I took him into
the room with seven bookcases

He grabbed at my tits
pulled open the sash
of my pink bathrobe
grabbed my buttocks
lifting me, pinning me to
the wall and was in me

moaning books came
tumbling from the cases
even Bukowski fell
from the shelf
as we hit against the wall

Ellen's brother came
to help when no man was around

LAST CHANCE

moon gripping the bay
leaving white fingerprints
on the water's arm

you release my wrist
leaving deep blue
ocean marks

we chose this spot to live
where everyone tastes like salt
wearing tongues on the outside
of their faces forever thirsty

you're not a fish or a shell
i can swim only tuesdays

i plead with the bay
to turn to snow
all we have
left is a sled

LUST IN 28 FLAVORS

for Guy

We woke them up again.
The couple who live downstairs.
I see their muffled, angry voices
a page of confused typewriter keys.
Shaking this huge creaking bed
like a Times Square New Year's Eve,
rattling the glass bowls on their hanging lamps,
we woke them up again.
Yelping at the Madison Square Garden rodeo,
squealing at the Greatest Show on Earth!
Tickets to every event in town
the room littered with programs,
matchbooks, a monkey on a stick.

When you're not here with me
I lie so still, so frightened.
I worry about us running out of ice cream.

Let's mint chocolate chip it tonight
or fudge ripple if you want to.
Let's rock this cradle till the plaster cracks
till the glass bowls on the lamps downstairs splinter
till the ceilings burst off the house
like exploding party favors.
The night will be so neon
that even the couple downstairs
will be able to taste the blue
and orange rooftops of Howard Johnson's.

FOR THE LITTLE MEN WHO'VE BEEN IN MY LIFE

the last three years
i have lost my interest
in little men.

a former champion of
the short & alcoholic,
i no longer crusade
for the equal opportunity
for the unequal.
i do not defend
those not worthy of
defense who exile my
offspring murder my
future babies, oh,
baby, i could tell
you stories of a
woman with so little
self-worth she perfumed
herself with vodka dangled
little men from her wrists
a veritable halfway
house for the unseemly

what ever happened to her?

she sold her jewel-encrusted
rulers, slides of one-inch erect
penises, sound tracks of alcoholic
rages, someone told me she used
the money to buy wool.

hey, baby, i've got to go.

i am knitting a sweater
for a tall lover who makes me
                        peaceful
i am knitting a house for the good
man in my life

THE REASON WHY

i never stopped knitting the house
for the man who made me peaceful.

furious fingers worked all hours
attempting a sun yellow a-frame

but every time i open my blouse
seventeen black moths escape.

voracious appetites they eat
my home until it is a teepee
skeleton of bright yellow string.

oh, home life, the internal workings are public!

i cannot afford to buy shades.

and the man, oh yes the man, who made me
peaceful, recognizes these beastly black terrors
but he does not know how to kill them.

LOVE POEM TO MY SON

it's not that i don't love
the kid, but he's got that little
chicken neck hanging between his legs
& i'm, of course, hostile to the male sex

but this morning, the kid, he's five,
& me went to the beach in jackets
hats barefoot we ran,
played, fell in the sand

& he said, "mommy, you won't have a 5-
year-old anymore 'cause soon i'll be 6,"
he kissed my lips took
cover under my poncho

hid under my tits &
smelled like buttered popcorn
i held him just
a little too long before
i let him go

THE HITCHHIKER

lucite blue eyes
fox tattoo on his hip
sun spitting on him
turned his hair velveeta yellow
his body bran muffin brown

always taking the curves
slow
i stop
to pick up
the hitchhiker

grinning erection in his faded jeans
gear-shifting fingers
sweating the electric
love of other women

my nipples pen points
write on his chest
(i know there's a knife in his boot)

back to an idle
in my empty car
i sometimes run
my fingers over the slit in the upholstery

tell me if
you see the hitchhiker

lucite blue eyes
fox tattoo on his hip
indelible ink scrawled
across his chest

LETTER TO MRS. M. ON HER SON'S INFATUATION

Tomorrow, the first day of fall, you
will be regimenting all your summer
curtains to closet dusting the Colonel's
bottles straightening the pictures of
Robin as a baby Mrs. M. here's
what you need to know me
I'm the "lady from N.Y." your son
spent four and a half days with hot
humid crazy hours children I've got
two a boy a girl who's very ill I
see you clutching your breast but
wait there's more my parents are Jewish
democrats although my first husband
died in Vietnam my second dodged
the draft and I'm older than Robin
thinks I'm wonderful I could drown
in his eyes blue as the bay where I live
in my poems beds of other poets eyes
of my children keep me on the straight
and narrow vision he has of me help
him as only a mother can do what
I can't let go of that gentle soul
search for the perfect woman
for him my love to you
and the Colonel, Lady L

LOVE IN THE LATE SIXTIES

i am a pacifist who can spit bullets
rip a man's heart at ten paces
shake the blood off my lace cuffs
& open the fly of the next
waiting man with my tongue

DENTIST POEM #4

He says she can no longer be his patient.
Her right bicuspid shoots fire like a dragon.
His left bicuspid is boring as a dungeon.

A princess does not wait for an abnormally
tall dentist in white armor.
She broods in the lily pond
her mauve skirts moist with
propositions of poets and skiers.

A dentist does not ride stallions down 7th Street.
Around his tan neck like teeth hang
X-rays of mandibles of women
he's drilled in his ten-month crusade.

There is no hope for a princess
with an insatiable need for laughing gas
and a dentist with an unfulfilled
need for Novocain.

There is no cure for fairy tale mouth.

DENTIST POEM #6

Easter Weekend 1978

The man who calls my nightgown "shimmering"
opens the drapes to the charcoal morning.
The Long Island sound ripples grey cashmere.
The texture of this silver weekend
fills me like an overturned hat
in an unexpected rain.

So tender is this man I fall
into softness for the first time
in thirty-one years.

I try to freeze whipped cream
and feed him concrete puddings
but he doesn't like things hard.

My need for chipped teeth
bruised lips frighten him
He does not understand
                    my fear of comfort
How it unsettles tongue, taste buds, teeth
even speech becomes difficult.

And I cannot live without pain.
So tender, so full of him am I
that I want to choose my own.
Whatever he gives me
I need to be ready.

Love me, I tell him.
Sharpen the drill,
wipe the crying lips.

LILLITH AS SHADOW MAKER

noon
Lillith doing ducks, churches, birds
shadows masterpiece shadows
on the headstones at the cemetery

midnight
lighting jasmine burning candles
flickering wall glows
she sways creates magic movements

he takes the sun for a bookmark
hangs candles on his key ring
wears a vest of lightbulbs

       steal the light
       pocket the sun
       blow out the flame

Lillith will make shadows wherever she goes

THE LAST LILLITH POEM

Sunday she called
her mother, ex-husband,
several friends, her lover
to tell them she was leaving
her two small children
alone she was going
to a salt blue world
a banquet of seaweed draped on their necks

Inside Lillith's head was a conch
which sent poems to her fingers
She placed her ear to sea green paper to hear the ocean

Her closet was half empty
Her shawls and dictionary were gone

Her mother said she was overly dramatic
Her ex-husband said she was trying to seduce the *N.Y. Times*
Her lover sighed with a stewardess and relief
The bay applauded her

Summers, strange unexplainable cramps
attack swimmers who sink smiling
A few winter fishermen never returned
from their mornings robbing water

If you listen to the pink
breasted shells you can
hear her whisper,
"Everything is posthumous."

EROS UNBOUND

1980

SOMETHING NEW

for Gary

ignore the cucumbers,
the strap hanging by
the bed, the purple
garter belt

i no longer scream
into pillows of
night auditioning
for porno flicks

the lightest touch of
your fingers around
my mouth pressed
against your zipper

& i'm warm & wet
for you like a
pie bubbling over
in an oven too hot

this is something new

ANOTHER LETTER

Bill. November. First snow.
Colder than an ex-husband.
Roads more treacherous. Ahead
of everyone, I've put my tree
up. Working in retail a life of
pre-preparation. Bill, I am
hanging the dated Christmas
balls, I tell you to make it
through another winter. You, in
Washington, your own decorative
global hell, you tell me
"I'll get by." The story of how
she found that woman's panties
in your shorts when you were
undressing, me in New York
trying to put mine on in public 4 a.m.
We need our trimmings of stability.
We need our back-ups, intrigues,
extra piece of cake, voice touchings.
Bill, I'm hanging the dated Christmas
balls, I tell you, balls to the season
of missing panties.

I CAN HEAR HIM SAYING

the woman i used to live with
has an ass plush as a velvet
sofa drove me crazy with hysterics
almost daily screwed around time
i thought she was faithful as shadow
day i left she told me everything
i never wanted to know who
was better than me in bed said
no one was more blind than i
never knew how much we'd hurt
each one did things awful as daily
news of her now i never want
to love a walking carnival ever
tell you the only thing worse than
a whore is an honest whore

NO APOLOGIES

1981

IF IT WASN'T FOR GENERAL MOTORS I'D STILL BE A VIRGIN

In a '63 Corvette
rolled and padded seats
listening to Ruby and the Romantics
windows fogged with breath
and warm, white sticky liquid
from the famous practiced "pull out"
whose quick and jerky movement
caused a slight concussion
when you banged
              your head
on the roof of the car
me having my lumbar vertebrae
separated from sacrum
by the gearshift knob
not being able to get my leg
back over the steering wheel
seeing police flashlights
while i in stirrup position
think
    with my eyes closed
    no one can see me
when the cop hands you
my red lace underwear
which was hanging
on the side-view mirror
You say thank you
he says "Congratulations, kid,
now get going."
we do, we do
we do, we do

CASUALTIES

talking about college, him
coming from kansas, ex-wives,
husbands, the kids, the time
we'd spent in l.a. & he asked
"what happened to your first husband?"

"a marine," i answered, "he died
in vietnam in '66"

he started to shake & blacked
out, saliva gathering in his mouth,
i turned his head to keep him from
choking, he babbled twenty minutes
about vietnam horrors & when he
came to, said, "i'm sorry, i'd better go."

i took his hand & led him
to my bedroom where the wars had ended
                and a flag lay folded in the drawer.

MOTHER POEM 11/12/78

whenever he puts his hand

                    in my pants

i say

   stay

away from   things you can

                         not finish

like poems

        about mother

poem   mother   poem   mother

                    sharp as

machete

       dull as

          philadelphia

exists

   in my sleeping waking

life betrays me

        spites

        degrades me

to every

     one who'll

listen she says

        my daughter

the gross humiliation

            blemish

on our spotless

        lives

exemplify
    empty

        bedrooms

      interests

feelings of warmth

        for my children

lightbulb love

      on off   on off

don't start
     things you can

         not finish

          like growing

up

   the only windproof

building in town

         shelter

strong immoveable   what doesn't bend

        baby

let the hurricane

       begin

WEEKENDS

every hot breath weeknight my bedroom
door is open to crickets, children, squirrels
embroidering my quilts and nightgowns

i sleep on busy pillows

friday you come by train

the crickets leap from my hair
squirrels honeymoon at the beach house
the children like laundry are folded into their beds

saturday the sun fries
you delicious the tine
of my tongue breaks
the yolk of your lap

the door of my bedroom stays closed

these three nights i open
to you like breakfast cakes

CONVERSION

for a jehovah's witness

they always come when you're in the tub
or brownie batter or mickey spillane story
and this one had such religious blue eyes
in his telling of the imminent end that
i began to long for a theocracy and in
this longing fell to my knees
and in this falling he knelt beside
me in this kneeling we touched breast
to chest and i could feel his belt buckle
pressing my hip and in this pressing
rubbing slowly rolling
oh rolling of god i
screamed all those pamphlets crumpled
underneath us sounds indefinable
escaping from his perfect mouth

RESPONSE TO GARY 1/16/79

bastard. male. cold-organed lock-
up. sit there. fool me. pennies
under your sleeves so your hands
feel hot. rubber bands on your
wrists so i feel your throbbing.
life-cold-organed-lock-up there
one hundred and seven miles away.
three hours. roller coaster hills.
accuse me! what do you think i do
with my days? inject my daughter,
insulin, 7 a.m., get the kids off
to school, drive 23 miles to work
everyday but saturday i do laundry,
magazine work, shop and nightslife-
cold-organed-lock-up even sundays
i carry cartons, answer questions
"literature on the right under w"
"science & technology left hand
side facing magazines" "sex education
behind me" life-cold-organed-lock-up
promising me what? beautiful-eyed
bastard at night i sleep next to some
man who's good to my kids and
tries to fool me never gets fooled
any more shit from you i want you
OUT of that place that realer than real
prison where they stamp my hand and
doors clang so hard it's like the
death of a child in me sees it simple
like the bay and how your mouth feels
life-cold-organed-lock-up what do you
want? to pay my tolls, gas, day off from
work, heart-rent after seeing you i love
gary i'm out here where reality is

more than the blood of a brother soiling
our sleeve as he dies next to us it's
penicillin, teachers' notes, frightened
lonely, empty eyes of my children life-
cold-organed-lock-up i want you so badly
it hurts. male. bastard. life—i want it now.
i want to warm you. i want you OUT of my
thoughts for a day. i want you. i want…
lynne

MARCH '79 THE VISIT

you tell me it's okay

        & i believe

           everything

you tell me

      i believe

        to be thirty

two years old in your arms

          is delight

full of you i am

       when i leave

          & your eyes follow

me three-hour ride

        home thru bear mountain, bridges, bodies

   of water

       is where
my house is

      cold laugh

        locked in a cell

whispering "innovative release"

      we glowsleep in separate prisons

PLANE POEM

for f.d.c.

Flying east
       sky ahead
              is whole healed black.
Behind me
       gash of sunset
              bleeds red as Washington apples.
Leaving "picturesque" Port Townsend, Diane & I
walked beach, town, woods, trading good words
              tongue & telepathy

Some things are clear & we agree,
Band-Aids & first aid cream are stored in the east.
Accident prone as we are,
              Diane avoids
rickety steps & the smack of tree branches.
She hides past injuries beneath heavy clothing.
I bleed & bruise at the whisper of thorns & splinters.

Ours is not casual suffering
              but a force of discreet will.

Hours pass. All dangerous objects have been buried.
The whole healed black sky has given comfort
to the bleeding out west.

Uninsured, Diane is heading for a new construction site.
I'm heading home.

I will stay away from French wine, the tingle of thin
white shadows & seagulls larger than cocker spaniels.
In New York, I hardly bruise.

It is dark now everywhere
              and we are landing.

AFTER THE RAPE

for my son, Matthew

I

When I think of those two boys,
                              I see you,
an angry nine-year-old blaming me
                              for the men
who leave your life.
                         Understanding angry boys.
                              Understanding violence
                         against women.
                         Understanding helpless mothers.
Matthew, we cannot blame the shiny barrels, melting
bullets, the spring that snaps under pressure.
                         We are all manufacturers.
When you slam your door,
                              I hear gunshots.
I am as frightened of your speedy caress
                                   as I am
of those faceless boys.
After months, I still cannot go to airports.
A plane ticket to San Francisco sits in my desk.
Matthew, I want to be able to hold you again
                                        but
you are bullets, blast, recoil.
Do not be angry at blondes, breasts, husbandless women.
Do not love sitting ducks.
Fight to be a moving target and escape
this shooting gallery.

II

George showed me how
                    to load his 12-gauge
looking down those shiny barrels.
But what would I do with a shotgun in the ladies
room at the Seattle airport?
(Tell your lover you've been raped; hear him
      ask if you responded.)
I am now living alone
with my tiny-breasted daughter, my pistol-packing son
in a house by the bay
where the lights keep flashing and
the ringing bells still scream   BULLSEYE!

TELEPHONE CALL

for r.m. et al

alexander graham bell was into s & m
not knowing what to say
my voice licks your ear through the wire
you are as responsive as a bird
pinned under the wheel of a mercedes benz
all the silver straws have turned to used toothpicks
when i grow up i want to be a volcano
this does not interest you,
though i know
you dream of a woman in pompeii
the next sound you hear will be
the bullet travelling through the wire
it becomes a boomerang
my ears are so terribly injured and hungry
the delicate smell of veal in wine & garlic
kisses my nose through the receiver
somewhere there must be a restaurant that delivers
or, at the very least, someone to pay
the phone bill

NORTHERN STAR

the magnet of you
pulls my nerve filings
to your body

       if i sleep with my feet facing north

you sit in yr cell
writing a poem about
the trial of a puerto rican
terrorist, victims of
chemical warfare or the
omnipresent impending
death penalty

& i'm alone quivering with the
memory of telling quinn, "fucking
isn't something personal; it's political."

the letter to the boy you call yr son
was read like a secret for batting .400
he sleeps with a smile

i cannot find words topical
enough to say i will not sleep
because i face surgery, losing
my house & other horrors you know

i cannot beautify my need or
marriage to a man in prison for life.
this feeling like the thick ash cloud
of mount st. helen's too shall pass

i will wake tomorrow morning
to the smell/feel of your
clean wet hair on my neck
& another sunrise pretending
a new day

for now i slip under
a cool blue sheet &
point my toes north

IN THE YARD

sixty-degree day in november
sitting on a picnic bench
leaning up against you
getting hard at my back
my kids playing hide & seek
with other children brown
& white poncho spread across
my lap your hands under
my corduroy skirt moving
your fingers until i rock
the bench & catch a gasp
that floats through the
barbed wire over the gun
tower lands back in our
ears tingle with the wind
i love your fingers wet
with all the want you
baby, oh, lucky i can
always forget where we
are under your touch

PRISON POEM #10

mommy where did i come from?

daddy & i are poets, sweet baby
& you're a living metaphor
written in sperm thru a hole
in my jeans in the prison visiting
room a cold day in january
in 1980 where we warmed
the living dignity & blasted
the administration's hope that
nothing survives of the human
spirit in cages of desolation

angel how we love even the
possibility of you

FIRST LOVE SONG

you know everyone's said it
and those with money said it
with skywriting, drugs & diamonds

something about us sings
not innocent could be
your memories of an oriental
girl with an unforgettable pearl
trick or mine of a big man
with jars of scented creams
                              but
we've got the cleanest hearts in town

love was born there for us
innate as the sucking response
& dirtied our pure blood pumps
like blindfolding yourself &
eating chocolate pudding
wearing white shirts

here we sit licking the sweet
stuff off each other's lapels
& all the years i waited to say
you're the ONLY one
vanish like sheet music
in the hot cycle of white
shirts being washed clean
the cleanest hearts in town!

you know everyone's said it
and those with money said it
with skywriting, drugs & diamonds

i say it with a song
notes running down my chin
onto my breasts
taste it
it's the first one i've ever sung

DEAR JOHN LETTER INSPIRED BY ECONOMICS & MATRIARCHY

they tell me i am loved
and who am i to argue
with my parents, children, friends

this is not a charmed life
but a dream vivid as the feel
of cock entering cunt first thrust

and still i go on
pushing pushing
against cool whip
luxury liners
locomotives

i will enter any tunnel
to escape
the bridges of expectations

the rails are on fire
the highways are frozen
people have bought me
too many tickets to fly

i don't want to travel

everything i need is home free

free pushing
            pushing free
home
      is only where
                  you are
being vacuumed from my life
                  like our baby

stay strong
          as the prejudice
                    of everyone
who said i told you
                    so i'll love you
always
          sorry
                    lynne

LOVE & SANITY

you tell me yr first
wife was crazy
about you push my
head in yr lap

you tell me i'm
crazy about you
sticking it to me
in the visiting room

you tell me what to
say who do you
think you are
the only one i'd let

tell me, baby, again
about you
i'm crazy and you
with bedsheet canvas
of our lovelust
are walking the line too

A GARDENIA FOR MY HAIR

i no longer need their hands sliding
down my hip bone
making impressions on my petal/cunt heart

i do not have to appear as silver vapor
in their dreams or an image luscious
but elusive in frame five & twelve of their film

i do not need
them to love me any
more or to feel my presence
like the ever persistent assailant
pursuing them in nightmares

watching flowers decorative & functional
in the lives of other women
no longer interests me

i thank my newest husband
for the gardenia
& pin it in my hair

INFIDELITY

baby, you know it took
me some time to do
being faithful making my
first legitimate attempt at 32
learning to masturbate
thinking of you

soon i became the perfect lifer's
wife you & i every night in my
bed head trips better than
anything real i remember when

we had this bad fight
i was watching the world series
at night meaning no harm
i've always been a pushover
for a good forearm

you know i've never liked pete rose
arrogant & ugly but all of those
good defensive plays handling that ball
i closed my eyes & that was all

it seemed to take & now i've
found i won't watch baseball
without the kids around

i'd hate to miss another great play
besides, baby, there is no way
i'd ever be able to do it twice
unless boston was playing
& i saw jim rice

PRISON POEM #32

"To love without role, without power plays, is revolution."
—Rita Mae Brown

i drive the long, dangerous journey
you shower, put on your clean clothes
& wait for us to arrive with books,
sometimes vegetables, depending on
what we can afford this month

i wait on line with all those
other women who work to keep
home together long hours
raise children strong as the
bars in this cold prison

after we've walked through
the four electric gates
our men will enter one at
a time we'll be blossoms
soft and perfumed and
bring them coffee, honey, sandwiches
they will warm the food, set the table

in a blur stealing intimacies
i touch you touch she rubs
he sighs robbing smells textures
to last until the next visit

sometimes i bury your head
in my breasts you find
comfort me in your arms
all is well no roles

in this love, my darling
all the pins have been
pulled from the grenades
no matter how long we
must wait we will
continue the revolution

BODIES

He really used to rule mine.
                        Undoing the
snaps on my white uniform,
                        pulling
the white stockings,
                        making me bend,
                                flipping me
like pancakes.
He was a cowboy,
                        owned everything.
The '56 Chevy, those ever shiny boots,
                "Even your asshole, baby,"
he used to laugh.
                        Ten years of not even owning
the indentation my toes made in wet sand
                                & when
we split
        I owned
everything!
        The debts, the kids, my own body!
My own body became so private.
I hoarded my itches, my tingles,
my longings   I owned them.
                                Now you.
A man whose body
                is ruled by the state,
                who showers with company,
                who's not allowed to sleep
in his own silence, shoot his load in his chosen
direction.
        "Even your asshole, baby," I hear
the cowboy laugh.
Bodies.
        Can you see us together?

76

the woman wrapped in a coat of velvet zippers
                    &
the naked man with a buttonless vest of flame
                        I can give you only
parts of my body   one at a time
as if coming to you whole
                            would be like diving
unconscious into a drowning pool.
You can swim.
                    Your ear, your leg, your cock,
they can swim.
Ironic to say, you're free enough
for both of us.
                    Bodies.
Can I touch yours?
                        Even your asshole?
Owning our own,
loving each others'.
Let the cowboy laugh.

PLUMP PASSIONS

1988

TARAS BULBA   FIRST DATE

in 1961 he took me
to see that movie
yul bryner made me
cry so much mascara
ringed my eyes i wore
blue black knit dress i
was 14 he was 19
got on his knees
wrapped his arms around
my waist knocked me
down in my parents'
stone hallway is still
there i don't remember
his name or face but
i never forgot the movie

THE MAN OF HER CHOOSING

This morning you woke
hard & purposeful & productive
& I woke with the recurring
dream of Aunt Mary's house, a
place I haven't seen or heard of
in twenty years. You had a walking
stick, binoculars & a guidebook.
I had a photo album filled with
pin-ups from the 1940s.

     This is typical.
     Hard work of the body versus
     hard work of the imagination.

What if today's the day we
can't crossover? What if I
can't see the plumage &
you can't hear the laughter
of the redhead in the Rita Hayworth
pose?

     In the greater scheme of
compromise,
       it will mean nothing.

But what of dinner plans, crossing a stream on a
moving log & the inability
to make our body parts collide in
any position?

I don't know who these women
are with hands on hips or tucked
behind their heads. Some smile up from
the album as if they recognize me.
The redhead is trying to speak. I

see her lips move.
You tell me it's the heat as you
put a cold compress on my head.
Something hard is on my thigh but
gratefully I fall asleep.
Hours later the ringing of the phone
wakes me. You want to know
about dinner. Fish or fowl, I
say it's up to you.

ORAL I

Her legs are spread
He is on his knees
She doesn't like this position
He doesn't like the taste of her
but this is an adult relationship
and he wants her mouth to
be tight and warm around
his cock won't rise
without her lips won't
spread without him
This isn't passion or
love or porno flick
but a treatment for stress
in twenty minutes they'll
be asleep her head
nestled in the crook of
his arm, his leg flung
over her in peaceful
abandon their toothbrushes
resting side by side

ORAL II

Her legs are spread
He is on his knees
His beard is drenched with her
mouth is full of his sweet
juice they swallow and
lick each other dry
& calm he kisses her
eyelids she presses
her hot mouth against
his thigh they sleep
stuck together like
stamps folded over
in a damp envelope
their clothes entwined
like hard, hot lovers
relaxed after hours
in a short stay motel
The neon lights are
cool, blue & permanent

SIX THINGS TO KNOW IF YOU LOVE A CONVICT

Never call him a convict

No one is interested in doing a remake
of Romeo & Juliet in chains & middle age

Five hundred letters a year only keep
you warm if you burn them

The more you give up on the outside
the more of a man he'll be on the inside

Underwire bras set off metal detectors
when you go through the gates

Love & Justice are twin sisters

LATE MOURNING

i don't know who this woman
is, michael, she's got heavy
legs & sleeps on her stomach
has sex on her back & she's
satisfied with so little she'll
eat a taco, see a movie &
sleep a saturday away she
can't remember a ski house
in vermont picture postcard
or breakfast in bed at the
waldorf nothing is spur of the
moment
she remembers the exact
date of every small detail
the first day her daughter
wore pantyhose her son
hit a double in little
league the day she met
her 19th lover but she
can't remember the day
you died without saying
goodbye i wanted to
say it wasn't all
bad those black, humid
nights we traveled to
the planetariums in our
heads exploded with
dirty release & it wasn't
shame
our last meeting
didn't go as soft as the
day you asked me to
marry a man who
wasn't a good father
is something i just

couldn't we meet some
where dreams touch
& you wake in a sweat
of recognition for something
lost goodbye, michael,
at last the tears
3 a.m. months later

THE OTHER WOMAN'S REVENGE & FRUSTRATION

isn't to call & hang up or ask for arlene
or drive by his house or office or bar hangout

the other woman shouldn't defy her role or his
she should make an art of pride & creativity

& accept the payload cries of his wife, the satellites
of indifference, the invasion of her planets

she should hire a skywriter to banner, "guess who
got laid?" over his backyard barbeque
send 16-millimeter documentaries of her happiness
in a pleasure swing to his relatives for christmas
seduce his adolescent children with pagan
rituals to disrupt the sweet family hour
embroider a black widow spider on the crotch
of his underwear to dance in the laundry
look out at her audience & loudly announce
his name at a poetry reading after counting to three
one   two   three
listen for his heartbeat

VALENTINE'S DAY, 1985

i love two men
this is not a new story

it's been eleven years
one is in a concrete prison
one is married

if god opened her fists
& each of these men
were naked as poetry &
free as nothing left to lose
& god said, "choose!"

i'd say i love two men
my heart isn't cut
in half but doubled

apples & oranges

this is an old story

PLUMP PASSIONS

i don't know why i called
you married a woman telling
people the reason was comfort
eludes me as he feeds my passion
grape fires, purple pinwheels
turning my insides plump cherub
cheeks magenta wings of birds
are yr interest years i've known
you passionless as a ruler
measuring counting numbers
of times in/out in/out in/out
until you've recorded every pump
in every cunt labeled juices
slid papers into locked cabinets
and here i am trying to explain
internal lavender volcanoes to a
man who lusts for ferns, reptiles,
tree stumps identifying only the
definable, categorizing orgasms,
infant laughter & passion oh how
can i explain they ciphered my
breath, my will, my adrenalin passion
plump passion that ate my friendships
to their mauve skeletons stretching
my skin to its violet utmost will not
let go to die its lilac death
i called to tell you
the deep crimson letter arrived today
they won't let my man out of prison

TO A MARRIED LOVER ON THE WHETHER

everything is tentative

if it's sunny you can't get out
early because she'll think you're
playing tennis and if it rains
you won't have anywhere to say
you're going but if it's sunny
you have a foursome to show up
for and you can only see me if
it rains but you won't be able to
get out

i understand

forget monday nights though
little league starts and if
it's sunny my son has a game
and if it rains the kids will
be in the house so
rain or shine

everything is tentative

NATURAL PROGRESSIONS

he bought a microwave
oven she wanted one too
but thought they'd wind
up together who needs two
microwaves weren't the only
thing she held back
purchases, proposals, points
to be made each day
smaller with less to fill it
he pulled back everything
was kept inside him
even bodily fluids she spilled
daily secrets he held
her emotional food supply
hostage she bought a
microwave oven to make
hot, fast, flowing
things herself but still
doesn't have airtight
containers for anything

FOR MY EX ON MY 40th

no birthday card this
year baby first time
in 13 years you've missed
one time we were the
geriatric romeo & juliet
of prison romance now
we're as cold as egg
mcmuffins in the
freezer section of your
local supermarket love
can't be bought but baby
it can be sold for the
education of my kids, a
loan for a new toyota &
the warm, wet kiss of
a fragile & kind lover
who takes me as i
am i so awful are
you will be fine with
out you i still sleep
alone most nights the
pillow at my back
is just a pillow you
said tell a lie twice
it becomes the truth
i don't love you anymore
i don't love you anymore

EVERYTHING I KNOW ABOUT LIFE

can be summed up
in just one sentence

he forces her legs
open with his knee
and before she can
fantasize about tahiti
it's over

DREAMS AS ERECT AS NIPPLES ON ICE

1989

CHILDHOOD MEMORY DREAM

i am seven, my sister is four.
my father has only one dime.
he puts it in coin slot for red rocket ride.
my little sister sits inside on cushion.
i ride outside on the metal tail.
at home there is blood in my underwear.
my mother screams.
blood & pain come from cheapness.
i am older, i can handle the wilder ride.
daddy loves me.

thirty-four years later red rockets still rule my life.
money always represents the cold payoff.
i giddyup, confused, in the space age
rodeo with the cheapest, wildest rides in town.
they hurt like hell but they feel like love.

APRIL/BAYVILLE/BEACH/LETTER TO MY KIDS

it's always the same dream
just like the night you two
left for college & i woke in
a sweat trying to remember
what i might have forgotten
to tell you now that you both
were going away on your own
it's never anything big like honesty,
independence, use of condoms,
good sense about drugs, alcohol
& term papers it's always some
thing small like today watching
the clammers in the bay did i
warn you about seafood or hiding
your money from your roommates or
always wiping your ass from front
to back when you were small i
hounded you on health habits for you
my daughter concerned about your
diabetes for you my son fearful of
whatever punishment life might hand
you two are beautiful, intelligent off
spring who have given me reason
for pride the seagulls are shrieking
in your little home village i sit
on the beach a cold wind blowing
wearing college sweatshirt what did
i forget to tell you? something's
wrong in my body and if i should die
before summer vacation what should
you know the reason i got up each
day working two jobs was to get you
believe in yourselves & become
whole, content beings capable

of giving, receiving what small thing
have i forgotten? the windsurfers
are getting started my hair blowing
like a blonde sail behind me a woman
walking her dogs are a responsibility
who cares for them if you work or
travel? no, that wasn't it. you know
the sun gave me skin cancer though
you both burn yourselves every year
that goes by i get closer to not
being able to remember what it is
i've forgotten to tell you. allyson,
don't sit with your legs open if you
wear a skirt. matthew, use enough
foreplay when making love you above
all else know how much i do you know
about salad forks, table manners, q-tips
for ear cleaning. one day in a mundane
situation will you turn to each other and
gasp she forgot to tell us? never touch
dead pigeons, be good to each other
& always dream a kingdom of peaceful dreams.

VIETNAM DREAM

six months after
we married in mexico
spent our wedding night
on the beach jack died
in vietnam unsure of
the lushness of jungle
love lasting twenty-four
years for a boy now young
enough to be my son will
never be a marine i dream
of regiment, loss, help-
lessness the wall in
washington i've never
seen his name appears in
black on one yellowed letter
i keep with my lingerie in
dreams we're sinking in mud
our breathing labored
failing to reach or help
each other touching
fingertips only

SLEEPING RETROSPECT OF DESIRE

1993

A TOAST FOR YOU...IN LIEU OF ALCOHOL

for Patrick Kelly 1939–1989

new york july grey sunday morning
my lover's head on the cushion
of my belly remembers the motion
of last night's sex frenzy bone
cold cream, cucumber, a salad of nerve
endings fed the haze i've walked in
all week since news of your death
makes me lust to prove i'm alive
your death, patrick, lust all the
more for how you lived artistic, boozy,
erotic late night phone calls full of
wisdom & humor i will miss you & your
cock drawings all over the house i'll
fuck this week wild abandon with each
thrust i'll squeeze out your name
PATRICK KELLY this week is for you
for you for you for you for you

HIGH SCHOOL SEX

1963

when dancing close was like
dueling getting pinned against
basement walls by the swords
in their jeans you couldn't
kiss a boy more than twice
or you'd get pregnant cramps
always in my right hand from
jerking them off in church
parking lot while they moaned
oh, god! oh, god! oh, god!

1968

in attic bedroom
of a levitt house rented
with five friends
lying in a single bed
listening to jefferson
airplane over & over
again i'm in peacock
feather bikini underwear
nothing else you're painting
flowers on my breasts with day
glow colors following the
curve of my hip with yr
brush can't convince
me to open my legs i
believe every time i do
my vagina will get
bigger my husband told
me when he left for his
seminar on diverticulitis
leaving me with concert
tickets twenty-four hours
of grace slick and you
the gentlest lover i never had

IGNITION

the shirtless man in the green
work pants digging in the gardens
at the arboretum
the woman carrying her wide-brimmed
straw hat the breeze blowing her pink
& fuchsia flowered skirt as she walks
something in his eyes, the sweat beads
on his abdomen, something in her
eyes, the tan line on her breast
she touches the zipper on his pants
he grabs her wrist
the nerve fires light entangle
explode in the greenness
of their one-time fusion

i light the long slender
blue kitchen match the charcoal
presoaked in lighter fluid will flame
the very second i touch
the stick to anticipating squares

like you today on the phone
when i said, "michael, my
cunt is so hot," & i heard
your breath quicken you
answered, "say something else,
anything," but before i could
speak you came

some things are like that
the green fire of eye contact
the blue flame of the barbecue
the red heat of the phone

WHAT'S GOOD FOR THE GOOSE

it is noon. april. sixty-five degrees.
new york. sitting on a bench. eating
seafood salad and orange slices
from plastic containers. she drops her
paper napkin. he picks it up leaning
into her. he smells the sun on her neck.
she lets him. he brushes back a strand
of her pale hair with his fingers. she
licks his wrist. he puts his arm around
her waist. awkwardly they stand up, drop
the remnants of lunch in a wire basket.
they go to his van. he never kisses her lips.
he kisses her eyelids, her cheeks, her hair,
her ears. he holds her face in his hands
and says her name. she lifts her skirt.
she is wearing pantyhose with a hole cut
in the crotch. she works in the accounting
department. she is practical. she puts
the condom on for him. he's an attending
physician. he wears street clothes and
a lab coat. they listen to their heartbeats
on his stethoscope. she thinks of her husband
fucking his secretary. "harder," she says
out loud. "harder." he puts his tongue
in her mouth. she sees her husband and the
secretary screwing on the office desk.
it doesn't get any harder than this.

TO A FRIEND AT THE BASTILLE

not all french thieves & murderers
hide sweet juices
under their drab skirts

grapes are the catholic felons of fruit

you are the bon voyage basket
a pineapple not quite ripe
oranges, bananas wrapped
with glossy green cellophane

who will deliver you?

most convicts have twenty-
six fingers, blue sandpaper
tongues a thirst that could
not be quenched by all the
washington apple orchards

who will deliver them?

this is not a job for the squeamish,
not for the acme meat market, nor
courvoisier, poets & writers, nor
the gypsy caravan of mutant metaphors
the salami sniffing gnarling dogs
of bureaucracy at the gates
will not let you pass untouched
you bruise as easily as georgia peaches

who will deliver them?

human contact plucks the evil
plum of heart
straight through the bloody ribs

who will deliver us?

raspberries are the elegant whores of fruit

i armed you with almonds & apricots
for the siege
your mouth an empty wicker basket
has been ravaged by the inmates

the pads of my fingers are stained
tart & blue
hang with me from the cherry chandelier
dance with me in the sparkling stirrups
of burgundy wine
i am the whipped cream dream
the cool cure easy escape

take it

ANSWER TO WILLIAM PACKARD ON RECEIVING HIS POSTCARD ABOUT EDITORS' ENTICEMENT

may i call you
bill me for a sub
scription tell any
one time i did suck
an editor's cock is
like his pen leaving
ink stains on my
mouth works before
my brain says this
is the nineties i
can't be a sexual
pretzel and a beer
at my place is over
crowded with poems
propositions you know
i'm an editor too
many men think blondes
with big breasts are
always in the way of
who we really are you
going to publish my
lips pressing hot
against your pub
lication credit
yr postcard for
this poem

THE ACCIDENT

the bus was as packed as a graduation
auditorium musty with the smell of sixty
teenagers tired, vocal, active like a
polka playing band on a music box winding
down changing seats, jackets, boyfriends
favorite rock groups, sports, foods
mile after mile the driver was
tired the roads were icy two
hundred sixty more miles to go
he was thinking about his woman
home painting her toenails, sipping
a beer, flipping channels on the tv,
fingering the elastic on her best black
panties, the ones he bought her from
niagara falls, waiting five days for him
to return from montreal, another tour,
another paycheck he wanted to rub
his unshaven face on the inside of her
thigh he pressed harder on the gas
the jostling had stopped most of
the 13- & 14-year-olds had settled
into their seats unpacking their suppers
the skinny, tall blond boy was worried
about history homework & enough time
to finish before monday when they returned
to school the dark boy next to him was thinking
about the girl in the third row her light hair
falling over one eye as she unconsciously
gulped her twinkies & chocolate milk
in its yellow paper container
the little redhead kept looking in a small
compact mirror trying to cover blemishes
& smile through new braces at the confident
boy in the next row who was throwing spitballs
at the chaperone who yearned to stretch, get

out of her pantyhose, shower, eat oreos,
watch the 11 o'clock news in quiet
was shattered as the bus skidded, slid,
hurtled down a thirty foot embankment
limb & torso stew, soup of fear & panic
seven minutes changing lives forever
anxious parents, disappointed lovers, worried spouses
wait for the news of who survived
who to blame who will miss easter dinner

music practice first kiss graduation
having babies mortgage payments
broken washers open-heart surgery
waiting for news of loved ones
after an accident
grief a bitter dessert

FOR A CONFUSED FRIEND WITH TWO LOVERS, ONE SUBMISSIVE, ONE DOMINANT

waking to a morning bright, brimming
with promise unable to choose what to wear
uncertain of the weather
is it cold as penguin soup?
hot as alligator eggs?
does she wear a dove-white ermine g-string
or ear muffs of soft silver fox?
cover her ample behind with leather
slick as a panther
or a flowing skirt colorful & light
as parrots' wings?
does she carry a whip or a jeweled collar?
when he kisses her morning mouth
does she fall backward like
an awkward kitten; spring forward
like a confident cougar?
does she bind his gorilla wrists
with electrical tape?
does he lash her flamingo neck
to the mast with sailing knots?
the movements the same jungle rhythms
the force of her hips provide the push
in a phone booth she can change
quick as superman
is she the mouthpiece or the receiver
on the telephone of love?

MARRIAGE

the tiny lump you discover
under your right breast
                    while powdering
the perfume line
he'll nuzzle moments before
                    the plunge
reels you back
the dizzy whirlpool
nerve tingle wave
that knocked
                    on your ass
in the first place
                    how happy
to hear the word
benign
                    one more
time dear down
the aisle of love & diagnostic imaging

STENCH

perhaps it's midnight
he's driving home
the road black as betrayal
he smells the fingers on his right hand
dips them in the lukewarm coffee
in the styrofoam cup from the all-night
deli he thinks of his woman
the one at home drying her hair
in a warm flannel nightgown
pink lace on the cuffs and collar
the only light the tv screen
the only sound the growl of the ever broken toilet
she pulls up the covers and looks at the clock
the other woman puts on fresh red lipstick
checks her sunken eyes in the car mirror
before returning to her own unsuspecting husband
she gargles ice tea with lemon
spits it in her driveway
cups her hand to her mouth
tries to smell her own breath
before she enters the house

perhaps he kisses his woman on her forehead
tells her he loves her watching
her eyelashes flutter slightly as
she sleeps he thinks of the other
woman's squeals her job selling
colognes he smells his fingers
again he'll be late unable to be reached
not where he says he was or will
be always washing his hands
smelling his fingers unable to remove
the long hard pungent smell of betrayal

THE RECIDIVIST

for B.

how long should she have waited?
dressed in a white sequin miniskirt
her long, graceful legs wrapped around
the thick, sweaty neck of a moneyman
the spiked heels of her high boots
pressing into his armani-clad shoulders

she was there when you got out that
first time hot and hopeful bursting with
capricious belief in picket fences happy
endings you got into fights, feuds, drugs
even the night i was there you came home
wet running from police hiding in a laundromat

every time you call it's a new bust,
drunk, halfway house, story the
husky, dreamy voice pulling me into
your jacuzzi eyes too full of women
i listen to the music of your movements
the smoky jazz swirling under my skirt

i thought she was perfect for you
don't want to talk about her anymore
she flew off to bimini, bahamas, bora bora
the fluff of her streaked hair revealing diamonds
big as vegas chips dangling from her ears
the well-dressed dealer, good luggage at her side

tonight when you call you tell me
any assault on a cop is a felony
you can't plead this time it's six
months sometimes before i hear from
you down in trouble searching for
breast of mother concern you get from me

she's gone and won't be back except
an occasional call late at night
when she's restless, unsatisfied
her green silk robe falling open
to lush thoughts of you fucking
her everywhere corner orifice hour

it's in you that itch that can't
be scratched that mechanical grasshopper
keeps your foot tapping, fingers drumming
all the things it takes to calm you
hurt you how long should she have
waited for you to stop spinning?

MEMORIES, MENOPAUSE & MALCOLM

you were born the year she danced
to earth angel in someone's finished
basement with a boy who pressed so
hard against her the imprint of his
pocket knife kissed her thigh

three decades later she buys
reading glasses, two boxes of kotex
waits for her period two months late
& results of a pregnancy test sitting
on a bench outside the hospital lab

you came up behind her whispered
to the pale strands of hair on her neck
she answered, "my libido is a deflated
balloon," but you took her hand
& led her to your blue van parked near

your kisses were hard as the young man
who hummed the beach boys don't
worry, baby as he pulled down her
orange hip huggers decades ago & cold
wet sand stayed the weekend in her hair

now her sensible shoes were off
tears welled in the corners of her eyes
your fingers went underneath
the elastic of her white cotton panties
she arched for you in that way

that says "i'm ready" you entered
with fingers removed them blood
red as ripe strawberries
"no menopause yet," you whispered
as you struggled out of your pants

"malcolm," she laughed, "sing a
guns & roses song," and the
blue van rocked in the
hospital parking lot for
memories, menopause & malcolm

SLEEPING RETROSPECT OF DESIRE

at five i was a princess
sitting on the plum velvet
couch in the mirrored lobby
of our apartment house in forest hills
a princess whose father sent her
hurtling down a cracked concrete hill
the first day on her new blue bike
without training wheels

at eleven i cut all the rubber bands
in our split-level refusing to wear pony
tails & played spin the bottle
with steven shapiro in karen
pollack's breezeway my waist
length hair blowing wildly

at seventeen i left the back seats
& beaches of long island heading for l.a.
where desire bloomed big as
grapefruits with every bob's big boy
i served bending into
a sea of glossy el caminos

by twenty-five i'd lived
the tract life widow, mother, wife
succulent baby love, emerald knife
husband love, breathless escape
with my children & my iron will
my dependable volkswagen
eighteen more years of pumping & pushing
against dozens of diverse bodies who
ever were or would be slow building red fires
out of control blue blazes until all
were burned to the graying stumps

stir the ashes with a stick of wanting

wake me with a hard-on, a heartbeat,
a helping hand, a healthy hump
wake me from the slump the sleeping
retrospect of desire

THE BURIAL OF LONGING BENEATH THE BLUE NEON MOON

1999

1960/SUMMER/THE SUBURBS

my mother standing
on a tabletop
under a yellow & white
striped rented tent
for david fein's
bar mitzvah swirling
the light blue skirt
of her spaghetti strapped
dress crinolines floating
like clouds singing
"if i were a bell"
from *guys & dolls* my little
sister hiding under
a table where david
& enid & arnold & i
stuck our fingers
in the huge white cake
giggled in grass stains
david's father throwing
ice cubes down enid's
mother's pale pink dress his
wife backing her royal blue
beaded bottom into arnold's dad's
lapping up vodka & orange juice
until we believed
in the adult circus
midnight the music
still loud we lay
on our backs in the lawn
naming stars & sins
we'd never commit
in the name of hot august
nights & alcohol

A DAY AT THE BEACH

under your parents' roof
you become a child again
parenting the children
they've become drowning
in the thick power
of the last moments
of their arduous swim

you're in love with the towel girl
the tropical oil she carries
in her little striped beach bag
her coral toenails showing
through her brown leather sandals
make you giddy

everything tingles with the
backstroke of passion
on the shore of death

afternoon sun & medication
transform the ordinary
into ultra poignant relays

you're always out of breath
out of sorts patience understanding
but not out of humor or lust
intensity makes you attractive
the towel girls thinks so too
she wets your thighs with oil
for the reading of the will

your parents are calling
they want sandwiches without crust
lemonade with little umbrellas
the sound of your recognizable voice

the heat & salt water exhaust you
yr postcard reads, "sometimes i wish you were here"
the towel girl licks the stamp before you mail it
summer won't last forever

LAID UP

for william packard

missed first step
fell eighteen more
leg tucking under
me feeling snap
hearing pop waiting
for ambulance
emergency room saturday
morning only female
in stretchers full of high
school hero football
season my favorite
goes crisp & orange
me limp & white pain
killers thinking of
your leg my leg
out of commission
until it snows blue
how'd you do it
for so long & not
go crazy ligament
torn ankle fracture
only two weeks already
talking to my pillows & you

HEADS

i owe it to you sometimes
when you're kind & open
i rage like a frustrated cleric
flames actually leap from
my mouth lightning twirls
my earrings you hide to
avoid my state-of-the-art
weaponry nothing can
stop me please i'm on a
roll over anyone in my way
more i hurt the better/worse
it feels like a hormonal tornado
ripping up trailer parks some
place down south where it's
so humid to lift an arm over
your head is heavy work with
me baby when the storm passes
& i bring cheese, wine, crackers,
grapes to your room you'll forgive
me picnic on the paisley green
sheets & i'll be so sweet you'll
think i'm the first woman who
ever had to dance naked on
broken glass & never bleed

TAILS

you owe it to me
when i'm horny & inventive
& you stomp your feet
like an only child
whose best friend
hit him sometimes
in a wrestling
match over oreos
you leave in bed
take your ball
go home if we
don't play yr game
the house gets cold
as a nose left
out of the covers
blizzard night
in an unheated room
you rush to me
thermos of hot chocolate
savior of orgasms
saint bernard of love
hug me honey bring
yr hard hula-hoop
of heavenly hips

DEATH OF A LOVER

i couldn't write
about douglas before
he was married
fucked me eyes
open hands held
pinned above my
head swelled deep
in me touched
something tender
as a bruise me
more with his
thick blond lashes
than his wide leather
belt buckle she
sent me in the mail
this week she buried
him at thirty-six
motorcycle accident
& wrote me he always
wore the inlaid mother
of pearl lips i gave
him engraved place
this is where i want
my kiss to begin

NEW APARTMENT

i can't escape
black canal
outside window
moon slapping
welts of butter light
boats puttering back
out to ocean
deck door ajar
wet spring air
thunder lightning
no room for me
in my husband's bed
he's tucked in music
memory of you
prying me
open to any
desire you had
i swallowed
lure of exotic
voice on answering
machine overheats
"fatal, fatal"
moving leaves me
exactly
where i was before

A SECRET

is only a secret
if no one tells it
to every ambulatory
ear on both coasts
she whispered
into the white phone
i heard from a retired priest
repressed hooker &
my cousin's stillborn
baby can't you keep
a secret is when you
don't tell every person
you meet on the train
restaurant encounter group
about where you had
your bare ass last
thursday the fifth
amendment i'm taking
back my intimate photo
fisherman's sweater
french thesaurus
sense of humor
trust me baby
i give as good
as i get

PASSOVER

the car is big
maybe a continental
cream colored clean
man wears a navy cap
flag decals on fender
woman a warm-up suit
expensive jewelry hairdo
hard as a helmet
he drives in two lanes
seems startled by horns
& today yesterday was
easier world war two ribbons
tv sitcom home kids
wife who accepted
perfunctory kissing
plunge for america
between her legs
scared of their island
home sinking in pollution
their children stealing life
savings heirlooms destroyed
by catastrophic illness is all
they talk about past & money
& money & the market
answers to everything
table set with fear regrets
soft medals of accomplishments
no dreams for dessert
there's a photo of you as
child on the piano nobody
who lives here was ever proud
of you clear the table take out
garbage like midnight on new
year's eve there's no one
to kiss for luck

APRIL FOOLS

lunatics in the driveway
her husband's upstairs asleep
her lover's pants unzipped
motor running her head
lights flash on dangling
earrings mirror movement
mouth full of his motion
moaning nervous release
she doesn't make promises
she can't keep moments still
spinning she swallows his sorrow
he kisses her sticky lips
searches for change for toll
bridge that separates tomorrow
it will seem like they shared
the same quick wet dream

WHEN NOELLE WAS TEN MONTHS OLD

she slipped in
yr coffee-colored
bathroom wearing
a cotton white
turtleneck cut
her lip bled
what seemed
like buckets
bright red
splatters your
pain ten times
her little swollen
mouth of my mouth
daughter now
you're a mother
can you see
years i stood
over you hospitals
comas syringes full
of yr life
i tried to
save something
of me
lost to motherlove
overwhelms
consumes
baby of my baby
make days full
as éclairs
for yr sweet
mommy daughter
of mine

RESPONSE TO VAN GOGH ON HIS FANTASIZING THE EROTICA OF THE CONTINENTAL SHIFT

"i'll tell you the animal
love is, van gogh," she said,
"a snail so small, slow & slimy
it lives in the massage parlor
of your inner ear.

it tries to learn shorthand,
vacations in miami & dreams
of a marine who leads protests
for a smaller defense budget

what we cannot grasp in our
hands kisses our genitals
as seriously as arms control
negotiations

tomorrow's children will hit
the cobblestone with new clogs
as we pray for their feet
to grow with ten toes."

SIMPLE

this is what
i forgot
joy
so creamy you
could float on
this is what
i crave raw
blind need
meat rare
as you
are what
i've been missing
love clear
as a menu
when you finally
put on yr
reading glasses
ask for any
thing baby
soup to nuts
i'll get it
for you

THE BURIAL OF LONGING BENEATH THE BLUE NEON MOON

she was thinking of anne sexton, poetry,
suicide, fucking, the long island sound.
it was raining. lightly.
she stood leaning against the ferry
railing watching the water. he was
thinking about his children. his boy
will start little league this year,
the girls will continue their dancing
lessons in their tiny colorful tights.
he adjusted his tool belt & straightened
his cap. she opened her mouth
to catch the rain. he laughed when
he saw her. she bumped into him
when he went for hot coffee. it spilled
on his jeans. she offered to blow it
off for him. "let's go somewhere &
do things your wife never let you
do," she said. "do you have a name?"
he asked. "compliant," she answered.
they rented a room. he paid cash.
all she knew
he worked for southern bell, had three
kids, a second wife

all he knew
her daughter married a medical
student yesterday a bride
today the longing a mist so thick
you could swim in
stream of pleasure
taking you to unknown
places you've been before
but not in this water
not in this boat

the need to feel solid
ground under her bare feet
sinking the anchor of fear
wraps herself in towel carries
longing in a wet plum sheet
buries it beneath
the blue neon moon

YOUR LOVER IS TOO YOUNG FOR YOU IF

he puts your pantyhose on his head
doesn't know the words to "You Made Me Love You"
thinks Jack Nicholson is old
drinks any light beer
uses inexpensive condoms
lasts as long as you do
was born the same year as your son

TRIBUTE TO ALL THE YEARS I THOUGHT I DIDN'T WANT BIG BREASTS

doctor, i said, don't
ruin my career as
a topless dancer
in a nursing home
day two i removed
the bandages
red scar
frowning inverted lips
sneering up at me
a month later the
indentation on my
right meat balloon
flashes its crooked smile
i am happy to have them
empty milk containers
heavenly pillows
mountains in a sweater
my eight-month-old
grandbaby sleeps
on the flesh lullaby
my comfort carriers
my headlights still shine

I WAS THINKING ABOUT YOU NOT COMING HOME

because the administrative assistant
with red shoulder-length hair
whose grey silk blouse
with missing button gets pushed
when she tightens her
belt after trip to the
ladies you told me
you can never say
no you don't chase them
but if the widow in accounting
with little topaz earrings or
twenty-eight-year-old
meter maid with full lips
in uniform style you
can never say no to
night it is snowing
yr decades-old car
could be skidding in
traffic or into a tree
i sit by the fire
& imagine the wreck
of this marriage stew
small white metal pieces
waiting for phone to
ring off my finger
when they tell me
you weren't alone
in tiny two seater
a redhead, a blonde,
a woman in uniform
i wish i never said
yes to the man
who could never
say no

WRITING

my friend leo says
it's okay to get
old & fat
to be remembered
as a blonde
dream carrying a rose
a pink velvet
ass bent over
a car fender
a warm mouth
wet as the tropics
all you need
to write, he says,
is the memory
he continues through
the phone wire
as you put yr
fingers under
the elastic of my
mauve lace panties
memory blazes
poems poems poems

FOR MY PALS, PENISES, POETS & PENITENTS WHO'VE PASSED IN THE NINETIES

when you live to fuck
with words you mourn
the death of every mother
fucker who sang lyrics
for yr blood pump painted
star-spangled murals on the
ceilings of yr eyelids
& when they pass
you are more alone &
colorless than the minestrone
of their steamy songs
are gone you long
for the frenzy of poems & friends
not another dead lover
another obit another lacquered
squirrel lost on the carousel
that moved yr wounded world

WHEN PASSION TURNS TO PUDDING

in my fiftieth year life melts
everything goes soft
hip bone hidden in my padded
peach belly brushes velvet
raspberry cheeks of my grand
baby, here injury air cast can't
help, i want to scream but yelps
have an edge & everything's
gone limp as earthworms
writing is like kneading dishwater
needing is like writing obituaries
people i've loved die often as desserts
what's to become of a tough, old tart
if she melts in yr hand & yr cock
is tapioca in her mouth
everything in my fiftieth
year goes soft & baby, that's real hard

THE TRANSPORT OF GRANDMA'S YEARNING VIBRATOR

2002

AUTUMN FAREWELL

i can only love
you as much as
i love all the others
& dear, there have been
many other than you & him
& seeing you frail beauty escapes
description when hard passion
softens like apples left on autumn
ground near where you sit soaking
sun you always loved the burn
now radiated by machine hearts
that can say goodbye can't be
broken by gentle kiss on your chemobald
head feels like gramp's after the last stroke
your wave weak as tea & i couldn't
wave back my wrist too rigid to banner
so long a finger puppet clutching
my cracked porcelain blue-tinted
heart in a thousand tiny pieces
i cannot form the word but
i can only love you
as much as i love

ETERNITY & THE GOLDFISH IN THE FOUNTAIN AT LOEW'S

don't be afraid of how much i love you

it started long before i was eight & stood
on the sidewalk, a river of nightcrawlers
stopping me from skipping to school
a pink fleshy bed of terror kept me
awake long into my out-of-control twenties

you rode in the backseat of aunt mary's
convertible at twelve when susan & i tied
white pearl scarves around our heads put
on ruby lipstick pretending to be grown as
mary's wild strawberry hair blew in the
wind we sped down sunrise highway
excited as bees on a frosted apple turnover

you wrapped around my dreams like cellophane
melted into the buttery popcorn in every dark
theater & every sticky seat i sat on the laps
of so many boys & men you lost track stopped
counting the times i rubbed the fleshy nightsticks
to their own milky, breathless madness

don't be afraid of how much i yearn for you

you were with me in prison visiting rooms,
hospital beds, the stockroom of a bookstore,
the lawyer's mouth i got lost in, the wrestling matches
of words & bodies at beaches, bedrooms, airplanes,
car seats, closets & my dark soul savior cushy
air-conditioned love, the silver screen

ease me now as our union is imminent

if there is no escape as i reach for your
cheek & brush it with my cold, salty hand
you've always licked the taste of me
don't be afraid of how much i love you
& where it will take us the cold dark movie
theaters where a single huge goldfish
swims into the imagination of us
susan died at twenty-one after the birth
of her second baby aunt mary lived long
after i am the only one left who knows you
take my crumbled, smudged ticket stubs

look, i am open & ready don't
be afraid of endless in my kiss

THE TRANSPORT OF GRANDMA'S YEARNING VIBRATOR

she lives in places her pillows cannot take her
grandbabies will widen their peacock-blue eyes
when she tells them about her colorful past
is a lavender balloon in the hand of a toddler
letting go as it floats towards gardenia clouds
becoming a dot on the horizon and lost mind
me, babies, live on the fringes of all your neon
nerve endings will be sweeter in a bouquet of hot
pink pinwheels sailing up to heaven's memory
filling your dreams like chocolate kisses & ether
this is a coupon to a catalog of sex toys & films,
a love note, a legacy from your maternal grandma
speaking from experience & memory's carnival

THE UNDOING OF MRS. LATTRICE

began slowly with a piercing look
how easy she crumbled his fingers
found her heart hot pulsing in her
pants pulled off so fast wet as spring
in her step strangers recounting change
her mind, her manner, her sheets
to the wind they rolled over past crime
won't help her now he owns her body's
manual flips the pages laughs naked
as old dreams slip away from any part
of herself she recognizes hungers thought
far gone as a woman ruled by a man who
knows just how far to push in push
out of her mind they are saying did
you see the buttons of her ruffled, purple
blouse left undone as a wino's fly? what will
become of mrs. lattrice now that she's
opened wide as the canals in venice? whispers
fill the air of his warm breath on her neck
makes her slide ice cubes up & down his
hard understanding controls her love
him forever she gasps, pillow over mouth
hand over eyes, blindfold over heart
slipping away she is undone

MRS. LATTRICE TAKES THE CHILDREN SWIMMING

in southampton on the rocky peconic bay
carrying a bushel of sand toys & sunblock
dragging the boy down the beach, the girl skips
happily white-hot sun bleaches everything
looking out at the water a skier attached to a speed
boat a dark woman in a white thong greases herself
with lotion spreads the blanket down gives each
child a juicebox their little cold, dripping hands pressing
against her flesh shocks her out of the trance
she thinks THIS is real life but cannot attach nerve
endings to anything but the brooding man who
saved her lips from cajun kisses & fumbling guitar
playing fingers the children cling like seaweed
calling her to attention between her legs a salute
to vodka & air conditioning & fingers
that do not play an instrument but
can make her sing a new vibrating music
with a voice she didn't know she had

MRS. LATTRICE, JOHN COUGAR MELLENCAMP & MCI

he tells her to call when she has
something to say all the time every
little pink house with red door mouths
swing wide tiny lives evaporate more
quickly than iced tea in arizona sun
dries spines rattle skeletal teeth
bite into what's juicy cell phone talk
until it's blue movies on white walls
to crumble marriages old dry days
without iced vodka pink arrows of flesh
pierce only what moves her lips red
doors open sound whispering his name
nine one one his name nine one one
"baby," she hears, "are you there?"

CONFRONTING TRUST AT THE DISCOMFORT INN

mrs. lattrice unpacks her bag
photos of all her ex-husbands
spill on the floor mr. lattrice liked
her helpless as broken wings
mend the new man said he could heal
her head rolling bowling ball down
slick as polished nails red as valentines
where he kisses she closes he tells
her open heart policy will seal her fate
brought them together she believes
all fairy tales he reads from his secret
skin she licks the salt of this wound
feathers sprout white as faith from his
chest beating her once mr. lattrice
made her swear undying trust obedient
as puppy love him forever don't let go his
dark blue beak still pricks the pink muscle
of her love closes her eyes his badge &
handcuffs framed in gold cold as divorce
didn't separate them even in death he grips
her hand back what flies free as the man
who knows how to open her now when
she pushes the holes of trust they softly
respond little wings of hope mrs. lattrice
loves her new yellow feathers
taking her high as lust in a penthouse

MRS.LATTRICE BATTLES GLENDA, THE GOOD WITCH & THE VICIOUS, LITTLE FLYING MONKEY

we're not on long island anymore toto
wags his tiny erect tail drinks vodka &
grenadine from a plastic neon pail glenda
sprinkles fairy dust with her pudgy wand
whirls around a warm wind heavy with her
charm them vicious monkey quoting yeats
at every turn mrs. L. to demon panties
they can burn smoke longing calls her
home is where a cock grows straight
flowering in her garden behind picket gate
keeps out bad boys, flying monkeys as
they try set her heart on fire yearning for
this guy she thought she found him just three
months before but he pisses on her sandaled
feet calls bitch & whore click your heels
together try to make it home is where the pink
stalk stands she yearns for the bone
goes limp well runs dry monkey tries to eat
her eye on your enemies as well as your friend
funny how eternal tale ends toto is rabid
has heart in his teeth finally releases
shredded red meat of the story which one
returns claiming the crown glenda, the good
witch washes it down blood of her conquests
all over town mrs. L. in pigtails gingham apron on
kisses toto's bloody tongue, clicks her heels is gone

THE BIG BLACK & BLUE LIE & STEVIE NICKS AT JONES BEACH

when she smells the ocean
rocked by music vibrating
her feet tell her mouth listen
to vodka soaked story of his
previous wife's penchant for
pain wells up in her throat filled
with him hard driving mrs. lattrice
can't say she feels embarrassed by
him discovering receipt of purchases
a road map to her desire a paddle
a pillow to bend her in ways mr.
lattrice never tried to make him do
it to me her mind whispers do it she
said no to husband meant it not to
happen twice tore her pleasure leaked
he hurt no good never want to open
again she bubbles hot do it to me
voice in her head again don't tell me
about another woman when you want
to listen to me lie about past experience
desire made her crazy as volcano
destroys lava runs down her thighs
i'm so hot mrs. lattrice whispers i need
you know what i want you to do it to me
oh, baby, she hears herself say hurt
me to heal me i know you understand

LUNCH WITH MRS. LATTRICE AT THE MERCY TIME CROSSROADS CAFE

the napkins were too small
to cover the stain on her lemon
colored skirt she spilled wine
blood red on the manila folder
holding a man's life mistake of
two minutes to ruin thirty-five years
of living in the envelope crisp cornered
by tight family job obligations slip
quick as a hummingbird's kiss she
thinks he will break his wife, children
no way to care for them pension
gone all for two minutes pursuit of
what drives us to nectar when we
can drink water quenches thirst
she sips from crystal glass removes
gloves places the legal documents
in order to make sense of time robs
us of what we deserved do you remember
h.g. wells was a genius who had his
crossroads & red wine nectar never
be thirsty someone wrote on the corner
of the menu in gold lettering she starts
a letter to her pharmacist, her lover,
her lawyer, her husband this is a
junction she writes i cannot find my way
would you like to order, the waiter asks
nectar? water? nectar? water?
her lemon skirt has turned to raspberry
her tongue too swollen to speak
she cannot swallow or choose or point
to the menu's little bold lettering in the
background mick jagger sings you can't
always get what you want at the crossroads
ask for what you need mercy her
eyes plead kisses hard as goodbyes

HALLOWEEN IN AUGUST WITH MRS. L. & TOTO

orange leaves are crisp cold
months away from loving furry
beast wears two masks one at each
end it now before her toyota turns
to pumpkin patch her little ones
play in corn maze seven feet tall
yellow which way out do you re-
member asking who do i fuck to
escape the costume party isn't in
october children point to toto say
here's my tiny heart vulnerable as
a shoeless foot on splintered glass
hiding behind mrs. L's big flowered
skirt over her head blinded by daisies
she sneezes love me love me not love
can't buy vodka or cigarettes where
would we be without hazes of smoke
& alcohol bandaids on baby injuries
save the autumn surgery for what
really ails dog with two faces one
on each end it now mrs. L. will be
sorrier than a harvest moon in august
over what was never had can't be lost

FABLES & FAIRYTALES IN WOODSTOCK, SUMMER OF 2001

he told her about the scorpion but
mrs. lattrice kept getting it wrong in
her version a fox eats a gingerbread
man when he crosses the river in his
tale the silvery fellow sinks like a stone
while the scorpion survives weekends
like this she's as dumb as a post a note
to herself listen more carefully messages
are clearly he's telling her to follow the
map of her heart has her confused but
last night on the phone lightbulb went on
the way to the bath she repeated he said
don't look at it like a lover you are my best
friends don't sniff like dogs her tongue
belongs on the strawberry cheeks of grand
baby not up his ass she's been true friend
doing the most she can see it today tell
him the story about the young woman who
sold her hair to buy her love a gold chain
for his watch while he sold his watch to buy
her a jeweled comb for her hair another
fairytale for believers in o'henry & love tell
him the one about the granny who adopted
a man child of her blood pump star of her
dreams of meadows of clouds no rent,
ex-spouses, battery-operated thrills just
lips warm as pavement on an august after
noon she closes her suitcase, straightens
her blouse says goodbye to love's bruises
her mouth says hello i understand slowly
gives up the pleasure of surrender how
trust made her sink like a stone like a fox
after believing the very quick cruel scorpion

SEPTEMBER REDEMPTION

she apologizes to her family tiny
gestures articulating i'm sorry
what you did not know hurt her
enough for you all will be satisfied
forgiveness bracelet round her wrist
small sharp stones to remind her
heart cemented closed played no part
mrs. lattrice sold herself down river
her loved ones camped near fire warm
yellow lit faces of those who trust her
flickering shadows on their cheeks
would cut like scissors if they knew
she'd come carrying umbrella holding
off rain streaks of pink sunlight peeking
through wisps of hair piled so high
couldn't wade into dark is something
you learn to love & live by feeling yr way
with fingertips break one at a time until
you get to ten then add black heart
tarantula prayers make her eternally unholy

MRS. LATTRICE MEETS THOMAS WOLFE
& UNPACKS HER BAGS

on her sixth husband's fifty-fifth birthday
she heads to the kitchen spatula in hand
waiting for splatter of grease to burn her
broken crystal wine glass to slice her dented
soup can to fall like the other shoe anticipating
obvious accident waiting to happen hurt her
scar like before she was deliriously happy but
water boils excitedly anticipating curls of pasta
with pignoli nuts, roasted garlic, spinach & she
whirls around the stove like she belongs to sun
kissed grandkids picking apples in watermill
eating cookies watching surfers in september
waves wash over last night's bonfire remnants
of flames made night orange as pumpkins
pressing against her husband kisses the top
of her head mind's movie theater never plays
reruns first features only now can she be content
feeling his relief solid in his pants & hands her
his joyful heart glad of promised return he hoped
she'd come back he said he didn't know what to do
but he does & takes her home she feels him inside her
all the rest fades old christmas cards in yellowed boxes
tucked away in the closet   all is where it belongs

THE SEARCH FOR ROMANCE

found me once or twice,
unfocused, turning clouds
into epic doubts into bibles
of yearning i ask my husband,
"was it you? was it this life or
another i stared into your eyes
& made you promise to look
so deep into me you'd never
forget these eyes of mine &
me, yours. was it you?"
i believe this happened.
this tactile memory as real as ray-ban sunglasses
the eyes weren't your eyes, dark as sumatran coffee.
they were greenish blue & i swam in them,
my private ocean of endless desire,
so wet with yearning my sheets
still damp decades later.
why wasn't it you?
the here & now we waste
like extra wishes on a birthday cake
noelle will be three in two months &
the unnamed grandson born in two
weeks, a nanosecond, a specific glare
off the praying wave in the yearning sea.
i almost never make eye contact.
no one does.
are you reborn in the flesh of my children's offspring?
it happened.
i know this like i know the boy's
heartbeat in my daughter's belly.
did i miss you? does it matter?
the search for romance,
this yearning,
survives tides of shallow eyes.

STOP ME IF YOU'VE HEARD THIS ONE
BEFORE

in the red weathered barn
standing in the hayloft
the farmer's burned his
wife's profile in a bale
of pale yellow
his cockeyed look of love
rocks the blue woman
lying in the gray broken
rowboat next to the goat
& the pitchfork in this there's
no traveling salesman
or farmer's daughter
just two women, a barn, a broken
rowboat & the farmer with
his dancing crooked eye
warming his wife by winter's
fire, milking memory of yearning
into a broken metal pail on its
side spilling back in the blue
woman's lap turning her
liquid to living she moans in
the night but the farmer's
gone his eyes dead as rusted batteries
she'll mourn a long time back
on the canals of comfort
blue woman grew to love
but not as much as she loved
that damn cockeyed farmer
burning into her his fiery ghost
alive as she's been in years
just from shared memories
she hugs herself, howls at the moon
this is not a night for tea with the wife
blessed be all the women that danced
with the farmer & caught his devil eye

SOMETIMES BAD POEMS

are like bad photos
you threw in a box
years ago the sun
light braised your
cheek hair appeared
too dark circles under
eyes closed midriff
showed pink today
you look better than
you remember yellow
rose & soft slope
of yr arm around
his shoulder resting
against yr belly
as you kissed
top of his head
cannot hurt or
scare you anymore
brown eyes open
the boxes & see

A FULL LIFE

for my mother

newspaper is full of them
obituaries from the buried
saints beautiful as pearly
ashes every one of them young
leaving weeping children unborn
& born holding american flags
i saw one this morning outside
your suburban home you lived
to complain not a day being
satisfied every hour whining
sad to have existed 76 years
without a loving word for anyone
but your animals 3 quarters of a
century how much can we cram
into the tiny clock of our hours
watching hands turn moments to
jewels of lovers names i cannot
remember how nice to have him
there 55 years paying the bills
taking care of what needs tending
your daughters have to work
something you have no idea about
fridays you'd go to the beauty parlor
run a charity bingo game needed
days to recover each week from
ordeal of hairdo & jackpots we got
ourselves into our stories multi lovers
faces we couldn't pick out of line-ups
more names than states in america
full life was robbed from those who
perished three weeks ago just a couple
of blocks from your grandson's building
your great grandson grateful you for
nothing you live like a greedy child
not realizing how many decades
your glass was half full

THE DEPLOYMENT OF LOVE IN PINEAPPLE TWILIGHT

2005

HER STORY

lillith was asleep on the job
all her dirty little secrets napping
he woke her like the prince in snow
white but turned into rumpelstiltskin

all men are dwarves in one way or
another woman wasn't the problem
it's daylight & opening your eyes
easy to love the smelly little fellows

still do love them all can't commit
one was never enough won't
be a one-man woman but will
mirror whatever they want reflect

obedient, demure, domineering
give me the costume in their eyes
see what they want play it over
on to the next man i love dead

men best can remain whatever
fairy tale they starred in no breath
no disappointment read to me
the one where the prince rides

off into the purple clouds white
horse royal blue cape ever erect
cock no voice box lots of money
a job where he's gone most times

now that's a fairy tale i can live
with lillith awoke from her nap
tell her the one about adam
give her a juicy red apple

REMEMBERING ON THE THIRD ANNIVERSARY OF 9/11

I

that day phone lines at the hospital were
out on the loading dock i tried a cell but
couldn't reach anyone my mother said
my father had made a train out of nyc
my son had not been heard from working
on wall street & none of us knew at that
moment how world had changed forever
grandchildren never safe i waited like rest
of parents everywhere & six hours after
towers fell i heard my son's voice he had
walked uptown to where he lived cell phones
weren't working river of people moved & he
with them after that day i made him promise
to call every week & here two weeks since
i've heard from him on this 9/11 i cry with
rest of america these grieving parents reading
names of all lost children where is mine today

II

lulu, i think of you at the WTC other wives &
how you rose to occasion yr firefighter husband
gone like tassels you twirled younger breasts
the beacon called him home & happy you were
weekend before drinking cosmopolitans him
watching kids are crazy but you kept it together
we cried as shock rocked family after family
crumbled lives we called our own grief justified
dancing on empty grave to i heard it though the
grapevine in november twirling your cranberry
tweed scarf over your head swigging hennessy
from bottle i tried to light a joint in howling wind
blue snow popsicles of sorrow my ex-husband
caught you before you fell & drove home
embarrassed silent moments at lake four of us
tipsy & life isn't what we expected to be old
on country porch flipping through pages of photo
albums glasses of chardonnay & tales of our revelry
now comfort evades you drink until unconscious
& i try to help you lost your children scattered
ashes are all that's left wave of your auburn hair
falls over one closed eye love you whisper in cold
pillow of remembrance grin pearlized plum
blush running down yr face to dead husbands
everywhere i watch your lips mouth his
name before you pass out of frying pan
into the fire i raise my glass & lay down beside
you widows walk lonely if it was only
as easy as turning off a tv

DON'T YOU THINK I REMEMBER

last year it was only
ten months ago i fell like
a building blown to bits
of it sticks & you don't
forget rides turn you
upside down holding
sheer peach blouse in
your teeth juicy taste
of too much sensory
overload burns circuits
& then where are you
alone in the dark un
happy once fruit rotten
hot hands sticky open
to anything but nothing
is what you hold air so
still mosquitoes sleep
on apricot dew pillows
you smell of insomnia
slapping the dead air
just for the movement

SURGERIES 2002

there was no drama
i read the report how
where what they cut
removed me empty as
colorful waxy box once
full of multicolored ice
pops up in recovery
touching the bandages
my life as a woman
no driving sex work
for 8 weeks i read
sad poetry e-mail
friends are kind & i
am doing well waiting
for my gingham apron
reading glasses cookie
cutter accoutrements of
the old lady dreaming
young men in tiny black
swim trunks diving into
wet that's what i want
again big blue splash

SAME OLD SONGS

you paint a picture of love
he has a name you know
his stubby fingers make you
swoon like teenage girls 1964
for george, paul, john & ringo
i want to hold your hand
innocent as your grandbaby's
kisses his mouth a player piano
melodies roll out no improvisation
he turns facing a woman beside
you cannot tell what he reaches
for first, you say, you cannot
be FIRST but you can be next
time you go home with tall
saxophone player he knows
how to make every girl sway
with new music every note
jazz, sweet stuff, different
songs each tongue kiss time

GOING UNDER

for spencer

we are in the pool
your sister & i swim
up & under bright blue
& yellow floats she is
a fish blowing bubbles
asking grandpa to hold
her wrists drop tan, tiny
strong body in the deep
end big splash she surfaces
laughing & asking for more
often than not you stay in
the background but today
grandpa grips your tiny arms
& lets go i rush pulling you
from the water you hate
up your nose you cling
to me going under the knife
this week may be the last
time we'll swim together
by afternoon you bob up
& down not afraid anymore
"look, grandma," you sing,
"i can do it!" & under my sun
hat i think maybe i can do it
go under not be afraid face
bursting through the blue
surface open my eyes &
you & noelle will be swimming
in your new purple suits
the pool will be clean
the world will be safe
i will still be breathing

179

IT'S DIFFERENT

now it's approaching seven
& the lines at local restaurants
are mounting you think i'll crumble
with desire to sit in a cushy booth
with warm crusty bread in a basket
running my finger down endless
selections of veal, chicken, eggplant

longing for a slice of cheesy pizza
served on the red formica counter
icy diet coke with lemon or a margarita
guacamole salsa chips or by the water
my favorite table bloody mary shrimp
cocktail garlicky scallops salad with
goat cheese & walnuts raspberry vinaigrette

think white tablecloth a wood-smoked thick
slab of steak buttery corn thai dressing
on fried calamari i love dinner out any
where drive through a few square steamed
hamburgers white castle of my dreams
our favorite pastime dining together you
think i'll crumble for the dinner hour

it's different this time i won't give in for
sustenance that never fills me i'll
gorge on dry salt less pretzels finally
acknowledging no dinner supreme or
endless with you can ever fill me
what an empty booth we fill together
does anyone know we're there?

BLIZZARD 2003

we came so close to levity
it was almost love

giddy with lacy snow kisses
valentines chocolates white
stuffed bear with ruby heart

clichés of romance cold
as thirty years can bring
you press up against my
back some icy february
nights it's enough to be

two old blood pumps reading
red-crayoned cards from grand
babies we adore each other
in a new way decades ago it was

hot as august sand at jones beach
now we shovel dizzy heaps slush
lovely as cashmere comforters
lazy blue sleepy flakes of fringe

we came so close to levity
it is almost love

NEW YORK CITY 2003

for r.m. with love

about a dozen
pierced tongued
short shirted tight
bellied loud head
phoned low hung
jeaned kids surround
us on the train
you turn to tell
them to hold it down
i place my hand on
your arm don't you
remember being young?

11 a.m. & i'm drinking
a frozen hurricane
searching bookstores
for an old lover's latest
editions he's dying &
not knowing what to do
i order his books he
wants no sympathy
i offer nothing but
relentless unanswered
e-mails to tell him
he is in my thoughts

& he is beautiful frozen
1979 drinking white wine
in seattle hilton
smart & funny
talented & bearded
one perfect affair
the kind you have
nothing negative to

say you know the ones
you'd repeat in a moment
smell of his pipe how
his beard tickled your neck

don't you remember
being young i ask my
husband on the train
ride home the thin tan
arm of a girl with long
dark ponytail & silver
hoop earrings black hip
hugging slacks departs the
rail carrying book bag
will she one day mourn
her dead lovers in paper pages?

how do we honor the people
we love them hard & to the bone
& now & like there's no tomorrow
& if there is we try again & then
regrets are a bill we won't have
to pay we live to love another day

SUMMER 2004

the man wearing reflective orange vest
riding bicycle with tomato crate on back
rolling stones singing you can't always
get what you want when do i get what
i need you now more than ever before
you went away promised things would
get better off without me dragging along
burdens of aging, ailing parents never
gave anything but mouth flesh canyons
for comfort me tonight as i crack apart like
maryland blue crabs with mustard sauce
piles of cracked ice melting on sea
green plates of debris day old love like
tuesday's halibut served on sunday
is this what we are left with, my sweet?
i do not want the blue plate special
break out the ivory linen tablecloth
polish the silver garnish this fresh
fish dish with lemon kisses & parsley
jewelry decorate my hot heart & it will
spill iodine valentines in your foamy lap

THE CHILD MOLESTER, THE BOTTLE CLUB & LOVE

he couldn't hide behind the pale
antique bottles & gentle collectors
ebay addicts & categorizers of
glass blob tops painted labels patent
medicine poisons milk flasks the world
of glass clear & case worn as the call
telling members he was among them
unspeakable acts embossed on his record
convicted felon tiny helpless victims heart
broken parents trust bottle collectors unite
what is valuable is agreed upon innocent
children be protected criminal be outed

when he appears at a meeting glass
heroes scatter he offers his hand
you shake it become shaken experience
automatic to glad-hand when one is extended
what has love to do with this child molester &
nightmare handshake that haunts you?

thirty years i have come to know you
& see through the shelves of bottles
aqua cobalt blue cloudy lavender crystal
clear that i love you isn't based on most
prized glass cylinder but worth of what
we know is flawed & make our most
cherished of all you show as beauty
& strength real love, my glass prince, is
based on accepting what is weak & loving
what is ugly unforgiving we are to the felon
generous accepting to each other clinging
to whole healthy pink bodies of our grand

babies may they grow untouched by wretched
longings & never see black hearts we sometimes
show them a world of random acts of forgiveness
beautiful innocence they wear as splendid crowns

NO GOOD DEED GOES UNPUNISHED

if we are punished for neglect
are we rewarded for being attentive?

my grandmother said if these are the
golden years, you can keep them

when she was 94 i found her in
her lavender slip hot water still running

face down on the gray bathroom tile
cold as a pile of montauk fluke on ice

i am thinking of being rewarded
dying in my black negligee

perfect makeup, blonde as ambition
shaved legs, mona lisa smile warm

as buttered toast the life she led
sweet frozen strawberry margaritas

everyone is punished here when we
suffer exquisite pain for unbearable

pleasure is the reward for being attentive
what is the punishment for neglect?

NORTH SEA/JULY/2004

hours on white hampton sands beach
dotted with colored canopied parties
swimming in shades of blue pool sun
squinting through lime summer trees
the smell of fresh corn cajun spices
supper & then on to fair blinking neon
lights games of chance ferris wheel
giant slide spinning huge coral pump
kins spilled popcorn blanket wet
spots sky opens fireworks explode
i sniff deep sunkissed skin & drift
back to nights in red convertible
after day at beach shoulders slightly
burned & the colt 45 breath of some
boy who breathes heavy each time
his sandpaper fingers try to slide near
yr untanned creamy cupcake of flesh
& it's all dizzy expectation & promise
here NOW the pressed bodies are my
grandkids' future looms large as fire
works july 4th finale & their cheeks
blushed with sun are the center of world
where in lightning bug's flash they will
park by moonlit sands with youthful fervor
creating memories of oily touch & mustard
smell one day they'll come back to this
night bubbling fries & bursting star dances
in arms of their grandma who was slapped
by the sun sent spiraling down to catch
their dreams of primary colors
kissing their sweaty little foreheads

THOUGHTS ON A SPEEDING TRAIN

when he entered her
his one-eyed man
read deep blue
graffiti on her
war-torn wall
she thought of broken
pink bicycle laying
in dirt jagged nyc
skyline something's
missing in them
in this coupling
of city/sex/motion
this year 2005 &
airbrush postcard
send to far-off pals
planet tripping content
as cows black & white
photograph with bold
orange lettering WISH
YOU WERE HERE
wish i was there or
present when i am
at desk it's easy
i close my eyes feel
him enter think of
missing towers passion
collapses like buildings
what's gone can never
be rekindled wish i was
anywhere but here

HE ASKED ME IF I EVER THINK ABOUT YOU

while we were sitting on the deck
watching the boats slap the water
drinking margaritas with yellow plastic
straws limes falling on my pale pink
skirt barely covering swirled gold toe
ring the memory bell & we are back at
the lake, the four of us, you, me, lulu &
tony lying in front of the fire empty beer
bottles in a green plastic bag remnants of
a picnic, potato salad in a teal ceramic bowl,
hot dog rolls in the dirt, bag of marshmallows
next to bottle of vodka & guns shining in moon
light like your very blue heart i loved you
more than all the others i gave up for that
feeling i only had with you safe as israel's army
i needed no borders it all was yours do i ever
think about you drunk car hitting an oil slick
smacking into pole holding your gun & chain
with my ring pressed so tightly in your fist
it left a mark like you did on me the ring still
burns & they buried you with those guns cold
& hot you used to say, baby, run as hot as you
do cold day i stopped thinking about you hourly
a couple of years ago unless someone mentions
undying love or sex hot as french fry cooker guns
as objects of desire & art i dodged a bullet & will
love you as long as the water slaps the deck
sitting here drinking margaritas with yellow plastic
straws you were not the one who broke the camel's
back & sometimes i tell him i do think of you

THE DEPLOYMENT OF LOVE IN PINEAPPLE TWILIGHT

camped at your tiny archway
lit by yellow glowing candles
sweet & sour as chinese pork
i taste on your full wet mouth

chopsticks red silk pajamas
slim volumes of erotica save
me intravenous they remove
from my blue swollen
hands in the midnight lime

light i call your name or name
i call your light & you appear
small screen on my anesthetized
brain me with yr club of love

where do we go now my rebuilt
pelvic paradox bops me under
wheels of progress rust like
tin cans in abandoned car
dreaming portland parables

pack yr suitcase solid meat
man of mine squeezes opal
earrings into my eighth hole
decorate depleted heart canvas

i am an artist's memory
bathing in pineapple twilight
kissing the troops of lust

HEADING HOME FROM THE HAMPTONS

they found her
one hundred feet
from where we in
a fog so thick were
lost searching for
belle's cafe on a
friday evening FBI
stopped car asked
"have you seen this
woman?" lost we told
them we were lost
hungry for safety
away from the onyx
drifting shadows &
across the field in
grey velvet cover
a tiny string of white
lights music sax drums
guitar woman's deep
voice of food so good
cajun spices blackened
steak crawfish safety
people loud claustrophobic
we found belle's that night
in the middle of no where
& now weeks later they
discover body in the woods
face we know grainy photo
we glanced in a gloved
hand through driver's side
window, "have you seen this
woman?" they asked & we
having no words then
have no words now

BABY BOOMER BUSINESS

knowing i should love you
& your glass eye in a jar
by yr bedside i lose at gin
rummy four hands in a row

you are screaming at my father
again for no other reason than
he breathes you spend too much
money cursing him as you wait

for him to die you want freedom
from his pain pins him to the bed
in the emergency room he can't
remember how he took this fall

the third one in as many months
thin as yellow pencil he climbs
the stairs refusing to hold the second
railing we've installed his pants too

long stubborn as a toddler not
allowing us to help how do we
stop him from commuting to city
again as soon as he heals

i kiss the top of his head
he says he's not talking to me
but can't remember why
i work 50-hour weeks & then them

this was sad when it was happening
to all my other friends their parents
fading like black & white photographs
falling out of old albums that held them

with the tiny white glued corners
mother i should love you loud as
cymbals in high school orchestra
you are too much noise not enough

substance i learned to love my father
very late in life & how to forgive harsh
neglect ironic how child once ignored
is there for you like you were never

wanted this daddy you tell me be nice
to my mother i should love her & her glass
eye floating in its creamy mixture like
these days i try to swim through

this sad swamp of caregiving

GIVING UP THE GHOST

for a.m.

did you get the card for the memorial
our friend, noel, "celebration of a life
most thoughtfully lived" what will they
say about us i ask you as we raise
martini glasses & light a joint looking
at photos of all our old lovers eleven
boxes in the decades we've known each
other's lovers cowboys, convicts, poets,
professors, artists, mechanics, doctors,
chefs, motorcycle racers, an indian chief
& an actor we never thought this day would
come as you are to the service for once
illuminating beauty but dulled by wind &
sun mapped faces once juicy as our sex lives
now dry as feet we cream with aloe & shea
butter me up with kind words praising a life
of thoughtless pursuit & dwindling resources
oh, but the sweet memory & exaggeration of
love lies in stories bloated purple with details
how gentle & obsessed he was, how virile &
devoted our tales become classic swill but
our mirrors don't lie look at us corpses in
training big red smears for mouths never
close the coffin & sing me a dirge wrap me
in gold-flecked red velvet use movie camera
to capture event i promise if you go first i'll
take the sea green tulle & sequined scallop
shells float you on a gardenia covered kayak
either way, sweet pal, don't let the legends
fade crying old lovers pulled from graves &
life to mourn us most dramatically queens
of poetry & passion may we live forever

DIGGING DINOSAUR DIGNITY IN ARDORTOWN

2008

THE 5,298TH POET'S POEM FOR A 60TH BIRTHDAY

summer of my 60th birthday
fireflies return with a vengeance
to light the dark warm skies
universe of miniature fireworks
not since i was ten & we caught
them in jelly jars have nights
twinkled with this buttery glow

my children settled with spouses
houses near the ocean what
more could a mother want
surf sounds of contentment

my granddaughter almost
as tall as i love to see her
bloom little 12-yr-old peonies
dance on her soccer-playing
torso strong bloodline petals

for all those years i thought
poetry was life
my life was poetry
& now there is only life
what a cold blue change
in my red hot world

wake up & smell melting
decades of lovers lost
to cancer & cross country
moves younger pussy
memory burns me to
them & them to me

happy, happy birthday
baby the song goes &
so do i

BLEEDING DREAM

just like the night
you were stabbed
& i lifted yr white
shirt drenched with
what i thought was
red wine the gash
so open it looked
like gutted fish you
let me call paul
doctor from down
the block after he
stitched yr shoulder
gave tetanus told us
rest i brought vodka
twist of lime yr arm
wrapped like sushi
roll me to yr chest
"vital signs good" you
said & kissed me so
hard for you to hold
above me faces close
i taste blood on my
lips don't stop so hot
glistens on my list of
top ten sex realities
i wake to dry life
no blood nothing wet
but my fingers in sleep

GLOOMY SUNDAY

a couple celebrates a wedding
anniversary in the rain at beach
gingham tablecloth damp with
wine & love limp as linguine

a mother in white weeps on gaza
strip israeli army pushes packing
hope & photos in pale gray boxes
violence now once peaceful mornings

an elderly husband & wife try
tying shoelaces together arthritic
fingers can't lace sneakers loose
memory trips them up like ropes

at local east end hampton library
we enter a musty room for book
sale & there i find you for fifty cents
bent blue cover my dead lover i pay

double loss this sunday nothing
shines pervasive mist makes
grief martinis two green olives
& nap on flannel sheets football

season almost here & the crisp
orange heart of autumn puts on
her black beret & sheds summer
clothes for suede boots of *possible*

STORMY TUESDAY

katrina has beat the crap
out of the big easy you
said you'd ride her out
but no one can hear or
reach you today streets
under water where are
breaks in the levee no
sighting from friends or
family looting no food
water hospital no power
news shows a muddy black
boot floating downtown looks
like your guitar is the only
thing you'd save silver ring
with cornelian stone i gave
you that night in opulent
harrah's bathroom on way
to st charles hotel we leaned
in lit archway sprayed by
fountain of light where are
you tonight safe on a roof
top or crushed by ancient
ceiling tiles we counted
lazy yellow afternoon hot
memory isn't good enough
get here i promise to keep
the one i broke if CNN shows
you on the road dirty guitar
case slung over your shoulder
red stone in yr good luck ring
shining like a tiny sun call me
when you get out & what you
always asked will be yours
words sent through sewage
baby, i mean it this time
can you hear me?
can anyone hear you?

FRIDAY'S PANIC

you're on yr way to memphis
woman with long dark curls &
ruffled cranberry blouse has room
for you to crawl under grandma's
patchwork country quilt nuzzles yr
neck smells of the road endless
nights a chicken leg in yr jacket
pocket silver flask hidden in yr boot
her out of bed where you dream of
stringy-haired blonde in new york
mouth full of you & poems & love
what you have bunch of tart green
grapes wheel of cheese & wine cheap
as dreams you sold on bourbon street
nightly yr guitar instrument of lust &
lies here under muddy waters deep
snapshots of drunken mardi gras gals
from kansas colorado new hampshire
they tell tales of yr long pink tongue
faded embroidered lyrics written just
for them you kiss belly to bottom out
& call the one who knows darkest hour
of yr regret to inform you of new
address in care of woman with long
dark curls & ruffled cranberry blouse
sleeping under black & white photos of
concrete blonde sing me a september
song of woe won't quit as long as you
remember her praline kisses & hurricane sighs

LATE OCTOBER PHONE CALL

comes on the night of world series
first game chicago white sox beat
houston astros time to go home to
new orleans you tell me cold creeps
in tennessee hills "keep me warm, hot
baby" singing it like the blues of delta
desire can't reach you there drinking
more jack daniels than usual words
slurred "shrimp," you yell, "gimme
cajun shrimp & red beans & rice" i
hear you trip knock over something
breaks her heart when you use her
best pink blouse to clean up barbecue
sauce "new york city," you scream, "warmer
than these hillbilly hearts." sound of
door opening & shrieks of big-haired
woman going wild glass breaking
laughing you say, i'll call you back
when you & i were hot as big easy
bloody marys i wondered 'bout the
other women tourists, waitresses,
strippers & housewives you swearing
i was the only poet you ever had as
if that crowned me special as sunday
sleepovers "please, come down," you
beg telling me about woman you met
at bus stop has a blue convertible lives
in tampa maybe you'll stay a month
cuddling up to her long, lean leather
reptilian body you tell me she's dry
as snakeskin boots you out & then
road again heading home, baby, you'll
call when you get there, "ernie's got a
dry place for me & i've got a wet spot
for you." sing it, put it on a cd. send it
by post safe in new york i remain truly
yours

204

NOVEMBER HOME AT LAST

time i spoke to you my father
was in rehab now another
operation on hip became dis
placed his skeletal fingers
reach up like ET's phone
home at last you are where
i can picture you can't believe
he hasn't eaten in weeks &
now there's talk of death how
do people do this mother not
willing to help me, baby, can i
run away will you let me come
back to you new orleans still
wobbly like eighty-five-year-old
broken hip struggling to walk
again i ask you let me come
static on phone line i hear
clinking glasses laughter loud
music it's 3 a.m. & you don't
hit the sheets until five songs
i don't recognize beat i do
say sleep sweet & let receiver
fall to carpeted floor me be
there this time when i need
you *not* to enter me like a train
but shelter me like a good beige
cashmere fur trimmed coat

SAY MY NAME, LOVE POEM 2006

i am riding the magenta missile of lust
my arms & legs detach from my body float
electrified into coverlet of purple exploding
stars i am nowhere **NOTHING** but a sensory circus
pinpricks of endless tingling entering desired
black space of **WHAT** i hear a voice in the distance
SAY MY NAME it says but i don't even know mine
the purpose of this exercise in flesh diving **IS** to
forget all but our bodies does it matter what your
name is whose son died in iraq on what side god
resides hungry children dead relatives daily torture
we endure as routines **SAY MY NAME** i hear again
& this is **NOT** what i signed on for fuck games &
giggles & going home without **KNOWING** your job
or child or sick wife or sorry troubles just your cock
sweet missile of pleasure letting me crash land with
out a helmet or address book to find **YOU** a man
whose name i don't know & therefore can never say

LOVE IN 2006

changes my mind all
by itself i read poems
on yellowed paper love
poems from men i can't
remember cleaning house
i stuff them in hefty black
plastic relationships i knew
were real losers poems
make me cry my father
dead one month & not a
paper kiss anywhere to press
my cheek against this brittle
mind photo his blue, blue eyes
vacant as empty closet dozens
of pairs footwear keeping their
slender silhouettes stuffed with
wooden shoe trees bare in winter
mother gave brown leather jacket
with fur collar to husband wonders
if it bothers me to see him in daddy's
clothes i never saw my father wear
anything but a suit & tie or tennis
outfit who cares who wears bandage
on her head my mother hit concrete
face first baby boomer mess we all
go through it makes me melancholy
wearing his gold watch she gave
me second job when do i live for
me caregiver me mother daughter
wife worker me after 59 years
want to be selfish me not different
from any other sixties' child parent
madness to watch our own death
on screen of their blank faces

HOLIDAYS

luscious sweet lip gloss my
smart lesbian friend spiral
cut ham & sweet potatoes
there were thanksgivings
happier than this one &
there will be thanksgivings
sadder than this day my
father facing third operation
in two months nothing seems
real story my mother fainted
what's next year we say will
be better than xmas kids are
gone to new orleans virginia
no one left here on the island
empty trees hearts pockets
we slice some cheddar cheese
open new package of peppered
crackers crumble like family
scattered pieces everywhere
love family glue drips like water
this year nothing holds

DIGGING DINOSAUR DIGNITY IN ARDORTOWN

the chimp wearing candy apple red lipstick
& an armani tuxedo warms rolls of toilet paper
in the microwave valentine's day is almost here
i love you daddy down in the snow-covered
grave goings on in the house you worked so
hard to keep mother an eighty-one-year-old
child i care for how dare you leave us speech
less parkinson's destroyed your brain & no sour
gummy bears or thick coffee shakes could bring
you back to all of us visited cried tried to help i
scream help it's fallen apart like a first marriage
bitter chocolate lessons you would be proud
your funeral was just what you wanted military
honor guard guns banging frigid snowy air white
valentines kissed the dirt & we stood frozen tears
worn like crystal accents tiny family together
accolades for you keep coming how pleased you'd
be a scholarship in your name me one to care for
mother dirty trick i can hear you cackling now
where can we find dignity of living long enough
for diapers & dribbling yr tiny mouth forming words
that couldn't be translated pain becomes ecstasy
as long as we suffer we're alive to excavate fossils
of world war two & ardor town we wished we knew
you when you lived there dreaming of mother in
her blue bathing suit & kisses you'd never imagine
would dry up faster than a wet beach towel in
arizona sun fades behind new york winter clouds
we miss you daddy gone one month we miss
feeling safety gone i am the older child & own
two remaining cemetery plots where no one will
reside in water is where i want my ashes how
did it come to this january weeping daddy dead

NEW YEAR'S EVE 2007

upstairs on the deck they
are shooting fireworks into
the water across the canal
someone yells "happy fucking
new year" pam answers an
e-mail saying we'll be sixty
this year i'll still take lovers
a vacation a trip to the hospital
pride in my children little poems
& pleasure at dinner & beach walks
the job photographs this year maybe
no one i love will die too soon or break
my heart this year is dedicated to me

JANUARY 2, 2007

i was emptying the trunk
of this morning's grocery
shopping sunny & windy
shadows dancing across
the lawn i didn't sense you
behind me surprised when
you said my name softly
i dropped the egg carton
& salsa in green plastic bottle
wind blew the crumpled paper
bag across the grass i didn't
speak but walked briskly in
house where i am cooking
meat loaf & potatoes tonight
for him the man i should have
left for you the man standing
in driveway on cold january
morning without gloves or hat
i'm not afraid of you or the past
or the future or him finding you
here in front of the long island
house how did you know where
i was a day off from work you
knock quietly on the garage door
i cannot let you in january 2, 2007
i have tomatoes to slice & peppers
to cook & a life like meat loaf held
together by ingredients that cannot
be separated don't come back
there is no past to discuss no
future for us it's all in the now
i must wash the little red potatoes

I NEVER LOVED YOUR WIFE

who gave me to her parents
right after i was born too nervous
to care for a baby she was/is one
herself still at 82 wrapped up in
own ugly world of wasting money
unconscious to politics of poverty
or love she spends more on beauty
shop pedicures & manicures than
a family of six for monthly groceries
how did you do it supporting her
sleepy days & shopping sprees while
you worked 75-hour weeks without
lust or reward your angry daughters
not understanding sacrifice for drudgery
is this it daddy your gift to me doing
her bidding, her bills, her shopping
you didn't save me when you were here
sacrificed offspring to her on altar of
your dying breath i promised i'd take
care of her your wife i never loved &
she creature cruel as leeches sucks life
blood from anyone who crosses her
path to hell is paved with good intent
on living lazy queen of sloth never
rises to occasion or before noon are
you laughing in your snow-covered
january coffin it's been a year i miss
your steel cold blue empty eyes

LUZ GARCIA'S HALF MOON OVER WANTAGH TRAIN STATION

we have paid our respects at ground
zero taking the train 9/12/2006
passing the cities of deceased loved ones
arriving to honor dead loved strangers

if what we fear most
becomes our destiny
what should we fear most?

spanish girl across the aisle feeds
pineapple slices & mango to her
muscled mustached boyfriend
11 p.m. heading home from city

he doesn't love her but she doesn't
know it batting her thin black eyelashes
like a latino betty boop leaning into
his tattooed body while he leans away

laughing with his buddies across the aisle
throwing unopened beer cans & crunching
potato chips carpet the train floor us as
we drag our strand bags of new books

out into the half-lit night the moon doesn't
belong to luz garcia & her party of revelers
tonight it belongs to manhattan dead & those
who mourn them like us spending a sunny

afternoon staring into the wide empty holes
an aftermath of hate politics that changed
our lives forever our children & theirs & theirs

if what we fear most
becomes our destiny
has it happened?

SUMMER SURPRISE

thank you for fucking me
at the doubletree inn with
urgency in a king-size bed
one shoe still on hottest day
of summer i thought sex was
no longer an afternoon option
ten months before my sixtieth
birthday & you come back like
ghost of lust wearing white pants
dark tan & eyes as green as envy
of all my friends who lunch little
rabbit salads while i eat meat &
marry my fantasies on crisp clean
sheets your watch dial bedside
illuminates dark drapes move
air conditioner rattles my nerves
steel reserve to never do this
again you say again i check my
cell phone a gray icicle in purse
slip on my beige sandals & head
for door closes behind me but
not you nothing closes you out
of my long love life i thought
was over you i am not

FOR MY MOTHER, INSOMNIA &
FLUFFERNUTTER, MISSING RABBIT

the worst part of the nightmare about
you being alive was waking up to find
you weren't cursing me yr daily exercise
shocked at your death you'd always say
"i'm so strong they'll have to beat me with
a stick to kill me," a little cough & trouble
breathing we met you at the ER saturday
sunday you were gone a mass on your
liver sent blood clots to all your organs
everything shut down i had promised
you'd be back home as soon as they
helped you breathe but they couldn't
i yelled "MOMMY, I'M HERE" & you
answered "i know" & then filled with
IVs & central lines & fluids you looked
like a thanksgiving day float in macy's
parade we couldn't recognize your face
my sister & i your grandchildren telling
you over & over we loved you praying
you heard us & knew we were there &
then not there just the year before we
lost dad to insidious disease thanksgiving
as empty as licked plates of homemade pie
your grandson told us they were expecting
their first child a missed blessing you didn't
get to hear & how you would have loved that
like fluffernutter, the missing rabbit, who ran
away into the woods becoming a peanut butter &
marshmallow memory that sits sugary on
our tongues mother if only your memory
could be as sweet

POEM FOR MY SON ON THE BIRTH OF
HIS FIRST CHILD, KYLIE LANE NEWTON
4/13/2008

a month before your 38th birthday
she comes early in april diamond
birthstone sparkles yr life alive
the way you did mine emerald may
of 1970 i couldn't ask more for you

than this grace of green velvet love
reupholstering your nights like a greedy
scarlett o'hara dressed in drapes
helpless we are to save our precious

children will lead you save you make
you ride the horse of an amethyst color
what you won't do for her this little pearl
who changed the hue of downtown dawns

quartzite pink skies & glass castles of wall
street king of kylie's dreams & mine
i get to watch this tale as you & your sister
& my grandchildren make this story your

own pierced belly buttons, tattooed lower
backs golden color, silver textures of dented
motorcycle fenders & peridot side trips
turquoise heartbreaks & citrine joys

finally i am ready for the treasured
endings of your semi-precious
choices granny's quiet crown
of wisdom i gladly adorn

TOO LATE FOR VALENTINE'S DAY

2012

SACK OF MY UNFORGETTABLE

brown paper bag of my mind
got wet carrying groceries
bouquet of carrots & one broken
egg on concrete along with clock
ticking louder than car tires over
railroad tracks the between mid
night & dawn hours my grand
daughters were born more than
a decade apart you sitting on
wooden railing with coffee mug
a single boat passes by & breaks
the glass of the blue-gray canal out
side my bedroom sliding doors you
looking out at sunset from mountain
top restaurant near taos bleeding
pinks & purples my son's voice
from cell phone walking from fallen
towers to upper west side 9/11
my father unable to speak no
thing but pain full moans coming
from his mouth frozen like
empty life preserver that boy
i worked with at bookstore
kisses made me dizzy
sound of him unbuckling
the belt of his faded bell-bottom
jeans one night in new orleans
big al singing sweating blues at
the pirates cove my grandson's
first words "read a book, read a book"
most electrical passion points
short-circuited until they all
are one memory i want to keep
leaking from the wet paper sack
of my mind forgetful hold on what

is lost forever like my dear friend
james, at 83, who e-mails each night
from his manhattan apartment
on east 54th with a list of what
he's forgotten

NEW YEAR'S, 2010

you disappeared off the map
of the electronic world
off the face of the topographic earth
off the postal grid
& then you are HERE all
i can remember is yr grip on
my upper arm pulling me
so sharply my neck jerked
silver chains flew & caught on
yr blue sweater a tangle of sky
STARS & then you were gone

if i lean against the dirty car
while snow falls lightly on yr
red plaid scarf & yr right ARM
engulfs me in a way i remember
from warm summer nights when i
could drown in the smell of yr musk
will it be different this time will i
be safe from spinning out of control
TONIGHT all my kids & grandkids are
somewhere in vermont skiing frost
on windshields logs crackling fire

places i should be right now i can
see your BREATH a swirl of white cotton
candy i move in for the rush of sugar
& lips i barely remember how to kiss
yr mouth wet as dreams got me through
so many years & here we are this evening
you pressed up against my ungloved
HANDS under your jacket this was the
year i was going to grow up give up

fantasy DWELL in home of grandma
solid & dependable as a range rover

memory is more than a FLOOD tonight
more than mardi gras beads & hurricane
hangovers in humid alleys of deceit
exists here on the island under this sweet
fake fur & the smell of dampened DESIRE
wicked winds rock the car & my reserve
for nightly news no lost children dead
soldiers HUNGRY families a city of jobless
a chance for better times far from ice
castles & slopes of eternal LONGING

LAST COLD LOVE NIGHT IN A BLUE CAR

always waiting for the other shoe
to drop on her knees to hear zipper
pulled open legs last time she'll feel
nerve dance prize of her body's pleasure
is NOT the doctor said abnormal results

& the tests begin & the waiting like all
her friends & lovers waiting like florida's
population all the condos & ambulances
waiting like all the children & grandchildren
for the ceremony that ends long after the
dying begins & the living dead enjoy moments

his hand in her maybe the last time she'll
ever feel the injection of dye warm as his
wet joy filled with dread & nausea clinking
sound of cat scans & rustling of insurance
forms her days back at work no doctors call

text from the blue car owner says call me
she doesn't sleep mass in her growing no
news from the medical group what to do
but wait weekend's here & now three more days
a rainstorm holds her hostage she crawls

into bed the rain beats the roof like
a drunken lover just out of prison

THE LETTER

today when i opened
yr envelope it reminded
me of sitting in green
volkswagen 1974 my
parents' unpaved
driveway my kids
then aged 4 & 5
raging in the back
seat while i opened
mail a piece of paper
fell from an envelope
like a delicate blossom
off a pear tree i blushed
as my little girl handed
me erect cock photo large
pink blooming tulip
inscribed by the sender
an invitation i didn't
expect yesterday
holding my son's little
toddler on my lap
second page of yr letter
xeroxed porn woman
on top her back to his
face his cock hard in
her spring surprise
don't get me wrong
i enjoyed it
bringing me back
to the seventies when
i still knew how to blush

LOVE POEM FOR LADY A.M.

a deck of greeting cards
happy new job love retirement
get well married engaged
divorced welcome baby
encouragement miss you
sexy invitation what's up

pastel easter egg colored
envelopes addressed with
pens & tears & crayon &
blood pump's history clown
who rocked your heart

limps off in the purple sun
set with a spaghetti-strapped
girl with dollops of hair
& not a care in the world
ah, to be young & stupid

moldable under the thumb
of starry-eyed kisses &
slobber of past romances &
comic book dreams every
man's fantasy paper doll
who doesn't dissolve under
his sweaty fingers & tongue

this is empty pillow broken
records little mind packed
suitcases stacked by the
proverbial door how the fuck
do they do it   break yr heart
from a thousand miles away

& as you take a tray of warm
baked goods from the oven
you wish them well let the cookies
cool wrap them in pink cellophane
send them off with a note

we all know what you'll say &
what you'll WANT to say
you've always been a lady
in love & literature

BLONDE BACKLIT BY THE BROOKLYN BRIDGE

at 7:03 saturday morning
yr wife called to tell me
you're dying to see me
unfinished business
haven't spoken in six
teen years ago you stole
my heart forgot yr voice
once made me crumble
like bleu cheese yr smell
captured me like a pirate
i couldn't escape my husband
yr wife called to tell me
you're dying to see me cry
at the sight of you hooked
up to intravenous tubes yr
eyes half closed you whisper
"blonde i can't forget you
backlit by the brooklyn bridge"
i take yr hand & yr fingers grasp
mine the way an infant does
instinctively i want to tell you
it wasn't me by the bridge but
you smile teeth missing trouble
breathing say again, "blonde
i'll never forget," oh how i
adored you broke my heart
remembers who do you have
me confused with my name
say it i say in my head but not
out loud living & you are going
quietly yr wife enters the room
tells me you're tired unfinished
business remains i hear you
mutter "backlit blonde" as i

leave sunday night 11:14 yr
wife calls, "he's dead," she says
it's finished but now not for me
on my last afternoon of breathing
i will remember you glistening on
yr norton atlas teeth white
as supermodel chiclets
forearms like a popeye cartoon
you are backlit in bayville
it was you, wasn't it?
i will say yr name

CLOSING TIME AT THE ASHES OF EROTICA TAVERN

half a dozen crumpled red cock
tail napkins rind of an orange
five olive pits eight maraschino
cherry stems one pineapple slice
empty glasses some on their sides
dark booth she sits photo magnets
torn from old refrigerator spread a
round her portal of visual doorways
she entered every morning taking skim
milk out for cereal packing half a sand
wich way out of the life she chose map
of australia, santa fe sunset, menus
from new orleans, ticket stubs, blue rib
bons tied in curly dark hair of her first
child slush of 1977 winter when ice castle
wonderland melted & the bay spilled
over like bathtub water suicide butter
white tablecloth spotted red wine
made her dizzy remember son left
with relatives & her sweater scarlet
with desire lay damp beside her dazed
like weekend she rode purple cock
of ex-lover while husband slept up
stairs she sucked off a stranger stole
her purse election eve will world change
on table crumpled bills & breath of jack
daniel's poet blowing on her neck tv
wild with expectation new president next
month's rent black leather jacket soft
markets will rise like the tent in pants
of man pressed against her wood-paneled
wall & middle east mania wars pieces
a new life starting tonight united
states of desperate humping its way

to contentment still she has no name
he has no phone number or family
photos or wallet or future sunrise
his face vacant as room 106
she showers smell of her own rising
croissant & zips her skirt lust gone
but hope for borderless country fills
her open nostrils with cracked dreams
cemented with campaign speeches
words evaporate like ninth grade
love replaced by clear yellow
morning the ashes of insatiable sex

A PROMISE IS A COMFORT TO A FOOL

Jamaican Saying

i never hated YOU more
than i do tonight
standing on our balcony
hurricane 48 hours away
sky a quilt of dark grays
spiritual white lights air
so thick you could pour it
on pancakes if it was sweet
enough but bitter taste of too
many years & a decade of sparse
longing for a man i gave up
months ago another promise
from you things will be different
fuck it i know enough country
songs but pity age & just plain
damn desire to stop late night
phone calls car sex sin of O
mission lack of dignity for
grandmother of six to be caught
all i want is peace place to feel
safe from winds blowing islands
to shreds of family photos look
at our all our granddaughters &
the one prince of a boy we are
blessed with i never hated ME
more than i do tonight
no blame for what we cannot control
not for inability to love the way we
need to be loved or the hurricane
that may make this poem yet
one more promise to a fool

LOVE SONG ON THE WAY TO THE AIRPORT

i love you as much as a good
night's sleep or a small bag
of chocolate kisses i keep under
my pillow in dark winter dreams
this is not a betrayal boarding
the plane this morning buckling
up to a man nearly the same age
as my son almost forty years
i've known & loved you many
bleached by white heat
of faded memories like the
photos on the window
sill of my mother's unsold
apartment vacant almost two
years now it sits as i do in
your eyes invisible & there
my darling lies the problem
women & men & aging grace
fully i know the chance taken
by wearing red high heels
black lingerie & boarding a plane
but you will not travel with me
you are afraid to fly, my love,
in so many ways i cannot stay
grounded to the house full of
grandkids & books & charm
i love you like climbing into cold
sheets after a summer's blistering
orange coiled day like my favorite
silver rings engraved with rilke
but i am invisible & 62 & do not
look it yet so drop me curbside
don't park the car i'll be back
in twelve days glowing with visibility

& hope you will conquer your
fear of flying how sweet if we
could be bold strokes of lime
green against the sky & see
what's left of this world, this
life together

THE ARCHITECT OF NO

the only word that spews from yr lips
the first response to any question asked
the way you look at anything out of yr comfort zone
the blocks yr world is built of/on no no no no no
to airplanes anal sex expansive landscapes
foreign films intimacy football meaningful conversations
automobile ride with no destination leaving a dirty dish
trying something new not giving a name to every tiny
thing burying yr head like an ostrich living in cell of books
& cds no need for human touch me by letting me go
why are we still married falls on me like wet cement
it's on me to say yes to freedom not to you saying no to life

THERE IS A BLACK & WHITE PHOTOGRAPH

of two little girls about 8 & 5 years old
wearing matching striped bathing caps
between them stands a man in a dark suit
his eyes so ice blue you can tell even in a
colorless photo his hands on their tiny heads
like a magician pulling them out of a top hat

in late afternoon he draws the shades un
dresses himself one by one he tells the
children to come & nap their bare backs
spooning into him who pinches their arms
shoulders buttocks instructs them to put
their spidery legs between his thighs

decades later after their father's funeral
sisters remember those times in the four
poster bed on top of the slick quilt with
grandpa never tell anyone & they didn't
for over 50 years until that rainy night
finishing each others' sentences identical

memories stunned at exactness of twin
detail flashbulb goes off their own father
never hugged or kissed or touched them
grandpa who always wore a suit & tie even
in hundred degree weather buttoned up
tight except those late summer afternoons

with his two little discreet rabbits
& their secret blue thighs

MOVING

a big bowl of heart-shaped rocks
from all yr hikes you'd bring me
one each time they stood for love
mica pink rust gray veined crystal
granite geology of a lifetime of walks

what to save from a dozen years
living on the canal water lapping
me to sleep against the dock of
stripping down decisions of what
to keep close to me in a smaller

quarters stones don't travel well
cracking most delicate treasures
of heart you put them in a box telling
me you'll return them to the beach
let other lovers find them there

if only we could recapture from
rocks what's been crushed lost
but all that is left in us from them
a large empty blue glazed bowl
SYRACUSE burnished on its side

VIEW FROM THE CHEAP SEATS

baby, i've got my flowered
scarf colored like o'keefe's
desert folds of pinks & browns
& purples i can smell you coming
down to me longing rears her
lovely hands decorated with
many rings of coral & turquoise

read to me i'm a pushover for
cowboy songs & rough palms
smell of cigarettes & booze
hazy memories of out of control
high school boys will be boys
but you're a man i'm told by

other women who've tasted
the alcohol love of your lines
knock me back to the cheap
seats gimme a cold beer & hot
dog ain't it grand this infatuation
move closer smell my hair stars

live there, you know, twinkling
morse code asking you to rub
yr beard on my neck move yr
hand under my skirt oh, fingers
of poetry make me moan breath
caught in my throat closing

to open to you & the view
from the cheap seats
where we can touch the
black night skies lost
aromas of youthful lust
dancing to forget

GHOSTS ON HALLOWEEN 2011

today i am in love with my puppy
who wants only praise, water, biscuits
to be brushed & cuddled in his faux suede
bed white & black whiskered face irresistible

ten years ago you wanted a black leather
jacket for yr birthday & i not like a lover
but a mother said it was impractical for
catskill winters even though you'd just
been released after 33 cold years in prison

what made me think of you yesterday
after a decade of rarely remembering
even my greatest loves i could hear you
whisper in a throaty voice one drunken
night when the room spun like a carousel
on benzedrine & i on my knees face down
could smell lemon shampoo in the carpet

"move yr ass back into me" the words i
say to my puppy as i try to comb out
tangles in his fur after i walk him never
once having thought about it the way
i did yesterday not sorry for past that

gave me today crisp gold leaves brisk
autumn air & six grandkids glowing with
promise i wonder about children for you
& how it all turned out 10 years later given
a beautiful empty platter & honed tools
for a bountiful life i wish you that my ancient

love thanksgiving, don't we both deserve it?

MODERATION

one of those scary moments not
unlike a week when you don't eat any
thing but pink grapefruit & still you
cannot button yr favorite light blue
jeans i couldn't remember a word
a word, it's happened before but this
night i floundered for hours empty
mallomars box by the bed, album
full of cock shots from ex-lovers,
over three thousand poetry books
on shelves, five dozen large jewelry
boxes spilling over with silver rings,
bangle bracelets, turquoise earrings
excess i knew duplicitous, origami,
surreptitious, inglorious, penchant
going through the alphabet didn't help
i could draw a sextant, abacus, gnome
word wouldn't come home to me
be grateful, i told myself, the word
wasn't "fork" or "grandchild"
"love" or "blow job" but all i could
do was wallow in loss of my facilities
we had recently moved maybe i lost
the word there a storage shed across
pond from apartment boxes of letters
more books, old bottles, extra comforters
it came to me i didn't lose the word
i never knew it

WHAT DO I TELL MY GRANDDAUGHTERS
ABOUT THE MOVIES & REAL LIFE

husbands punch their wives after beers
with the boys losing at cards or racetrack
they come home smelling like sachet from
lingerie drawer not yours checkbook lost while
kayaking glue themselves to their glasses
cheaters, brutes, idiots, sissies they kiss
or beat the crap out of their respective
spouses who are all unfaithful blondes
with great tits & ass acting cool as blue
plastic ice cube trays or brunettes in
pale pink cashmere & nylon stockings
cheeks peachy as produce from augusta

get grade A education love your limbs like
branches of the weeping willow write poems
in linen clouds dance like a vengeful rain
hump like sweet bunnies paint canvases big
as arizona canyons travel the world ten times
over paint yr lips & cheeks with pomegranate
kiss the lower back of any human who shares
yr joyful pain & macro photography don't ever
care what others think of yourselves as warrior
princesses deserving of the universe & own it

SAFETY

is not found in the crook of yr pale
boney armpit slight light gray hairs
& faint smell of soupy wooly sweat

how i clung to the cave of his dark
muscular shoulder curls of black fur
gripping me like mink champagne

i fend for myself now & own my oven
rising desire & flakey turnover tales
odors rule the kitchen & bedroom

winter is here for barren good or bad
lilac blossom lust & raspberry peach
spring pies won't ever come again

danger lurks in the potpourri of my
love i carry a 9 mm glock & sage
scented candles in my summer purse

NEW POEMS

2012–2013

ANOTHER DREAM

as instructed by you
before sleep i thought
of ryan gosling shirtless
but he did not appear
in my nighttime illusions
instead sitting on large rock
eating peanut butter & jelly
sandwich an old man in
marine blue t-shirt gourmet
grilled chicken chipotle
bacon avocado club i
made him at 4 a.m. lay
in mud which only goes to
prove yr instructions don't
always work & my efforts
for creative pleasure seem
to have hit the unpaved road
sleep may not be path to
my satisfaction but the old
man is doing just fine

MY FRIEND SAYS HE HAS SEX EVERY TIME

it rains water dances stop his demo saw
from cutting bluestone for walls & walkways
his woman watches weather forecasts & comes
bringing food in little white paper containers
& a yellow flowered umbrella with a red handle

years ago when i had sex with him it wasn't
dependent on weeping clouds i brought johnny
walker black label & can't remember much about
those warm afternoons or air conditioned nights
mornings we woke with headaches bright as oranges

more than a decade later we speak on the phone hours
catching up on missed years of joy, baseball, lovers, slices
of pain, poems, films, kids mundane opportunities for a
throaty laugh or floating clouds of the time he did that brought
us together my name tattooed on his arm faded as the lust

that used to drive me to him like oxycodone love drugs
a thing of the past grown-up friendship replaces now
our pumps get primed by younger flesh & fantasies
timing is the key to everything & ours was always off
comfortable as blue velvet memory foam–lined slippers

we wear each other well

WHEN WE CAN'T HAVE EVERYTHING

we settle for what we can gratefully
carry in domestic overnight flight bag

how much i love you is no longer
predicated on how little i am loved
by someone else calls at midnight

i don't always recognize voice
but i identify need specific as
boarding pass with proper ID

maybe yr women weren't chosen
for who they were but forced to
change into what you would have

them be careful what you wish for
old saying goes you taught me to
tell the difference now it's my turn

to teach you departures arrivals
may not often be on time but if you
are waiting by the gate chances

of blissful reconnection complete with
swooning kisses becomes possible

THE PAST AS HOUSEGUEST

is staying quietly in the back bedroom
we invite him out on evenings when
air thick as upholstery weighs on us
he brings a joyful breeze & broken
carnival lights to remind us nothing

is as bad or good as we remember
soft lips of a once gentle lover harsh
criticism slaps blade of kitchen knife
baby's breath flower or human lace
tastes as sweet as ripe nectarines

my sister says we are like our mother
who spent her life pining for college
beau & at 83 years old still searched
for him on the internet under retired

professors no i tell sister recall
long lists of men who pursued us
joints big as cigars trips black bras
backseats good meals bad lays not
the same as mother's undone fantasy

we've lived & earned the right to invite
past to sit at table tonight eat up i tell
him have some red wine all too soon you
must return to your sequestered bedroom
listen to ceiling fan whine softly wait

until the next time we invite you
to be part of the repast of the present

THE GOOD LETTERS

are what she called them
back in the day when he
was locked up & she lived
only for his paper touch
rare press of flesh which
most times escaped them

good letters were not full of
family details daily routines
declarations of undying love
one of them knew wouldn't
last forever she believed hot
future rocking chair memory

what he would do to her
she wanted to do for him
breath rapid when reading
words became tongue cunt
cock pen wrote her wet
dreams satisfying as bubbly

champagne of her masturbatory
fantasies he reigned with belt
she with vibrating toys lotions
another way to communicate
he said part of us she shredded
saving her survivors' vivid visions

good letters she wished now
she'd kept just one

SEVERE THUNDERSTORMS, BROKEN PROMISES

yr woman braved rains came soaking
wet with soggy pizza box & needs
hair black as crow's feathers drape pillow
she bends over water swirls outside

two hundred miles away my lover
calls from cell phone stuck on long
island expressway lightning rivers
of rain windshield wipers singsong

broken promises spill over drainpipe

sun expected by midday too late for
me to fluff cushions change sheets
go back to city i tell my southern pal
driving rain leaves a small dark window

broken promises spill over drainpipe

my dog likes to watch slanted driven
showers he growls at swans in pond
melted sugar doughnut by coffee cup
left husband says it's never too late

love is for idiots & liars & the young
i don't deliver food or sex or medical
care come to me for advice i am always
matriarch sometimes confused honest

promises fill my weekend purse
due to weather i remain true
to everything i've ever told you
i hang on heart & guitar string

MRS. LATTRICE IN THE LOOKING GLASS

darlin' remember the rabbit
hole as you skate on greener
grass pastures of pleasure need
manure to shine emerald love

carry yr fine lizard purse down
to new orleans where drowned
dreams are resurrected by hand
of man who's been through it all

three of his calloused fingers in
yr magnolia suitcase & the south
will overflow like lake pontchartrain
happy home of lust waterways

up north there are hardened hearts
veined with silver rivers running dry
as hampton sands in jumpin' july
what's behind tangerine striped tent

number three choice was made for
you over a decade ago it's all over
now accept the closure of bank accounts
who gets the puppy book cock collection

sleep on wrinkled sheets fry an egg
with hot sauce listen to his new lyrics
as he strums guitar naked except for
his boots cell phone full of new numbers

who can count backwards to one hundred
ninety nine ninety eight ninety seven
times pink veined stalks equal loveless
garden mrs. lattrice wears big straw sun

hat in hand where will she land?

FOR PAST LOVER FOR WHOM I HAVE CURRENT

sexual attraction i am sending you
photo of my right thigh always least
favorite part of my body looking back
bent over mirror my ass is holding up
well may i gratefully implore you send

me photo of body part attached to
you i should see before i continue
fantasizing slap of sex helping this
old gal sleep like contented toddler

ah, smell of you draws me like old
furniture sold after we spilled on
armchairs & beds & shower juice
of lust ragged as broken wine bottle

senior citizens of desire i lick
thoughts of you fill me with easy
breathing mental ambien no pills
can we bottle this for baby boomers
love, we'd be richer than our happy

hardening arteries diamond hearts

MRS. LATTRICE'S HOLIDAY WEEKEND DISASTER

air conditioning fails like nervous high school
student day of SATs she spread herself open
as hot turkey sandwich towels to cover bed
astroglide array of vibrating toys anal porn

arranged a smorgasbord of happy afternoon
to come not once but dozens of times just
thinking about him inhale cigarette hear
pause between "baby" & "you can do it" she

can see look of amusement in his eyes though
he isn't there just his voice on phone enough to
make her shy & shaken like salt on over easy
morning eggs she has showered no makeup

memories of when they were fucking motel
dark deliriously cold no future only past
but now no past future only present is where
she lives at her age every day a gift to be savored

shot of vodka hides any remaining inhibitions
she may have harbored him in all her places
that count cunt mouth ass let him have her
heart if that's what it takes to keep feeling alive

new orleans just two weeks away she knows
what waits there is honest as three-year-old
on santa's lap what do you want little girl
mrs. lattrice accepts candy cane from jolly

man & sucks & sucks & sucks as she ponders
question what is real & what evaporates like
sweat between her breasts when air conditioner
finally starts its beautiful hum again

JOHN MUIR FOREST OF LOVE

he tells me love takes up space
"there's not a thimble of it where
you live" he insists infinite
emptiness sleeps in my bed

i want to measure love now
to know how big my house
must be to share it with him
for whom my lust is voluminous

he doesn't understand
love hides here in a way
it can't be found maybe
in storage space packed
suitcase from past trips new
orleans, santa fe, san francisco

i admit to walking through home
halls as cold as meat freezers
i admit to phone calls sizzling
as barbeque pits & just as filling

torn between hungers that can
& cannot be filled i lick my fingers
one hand cold & dry as empty grape
stem one hand sweet & wet as plump
red cherries i need two hands

to function & yet here i sit
typing with confused stumps
like oversized thimbles

THANKSGIVING 2012

i love two men
this is not a new story

it's been forty years
one spent thirty-three years
in prison one i am married to

if god opened her fists
& i was free & naked as
poetry with nothing left
to lose & god said, "choose!"

i'd say i love two men
my heart isn't cut
in half but doubled

apples & oranges

this is a never-ending story

MRS. LATTRICE WRITES A LETTER ON THE FOURTH OF JULY

my dearest, mr. x., i stood on balcony for only five hot
minutes fireworks balleted across the pond above trees
colorful as neon streamers but all i wanted to see was
top of yr head buried between my breasts & smell humid
summer lust covering us like veil of age we now carry

it may be unfair to speak of my longings these summer
evenings find me dreaming of yr rough hands gentle
lips, oh, may i distinguish you from many other lovers
head of yr cock pushing between my cheeks i blush
at thoughts of us blooming in me like late spring

this, i must tell you, my love, i want to swallow you
hungrily as an unfed animal after a winter's fast i
am insatiable but it is my heart that hungers now
for the tiniest of treasures small measures of
domesticity years have robbed from us

please, mr. x., i apologize for this flight of fancy
this fantasy where i drop my flowery skirts & blood
pump in puddle at yr feet i kneel to serve there is
no coming back from where i have been taken how
silly to profess my love like schoolgirls i lecture

my cheeks flush like fallen peaches each evening
without shame i rise to you with my own fingers
wishing them to be yrs as i am everlasting imbecile
they say there is no fool like an old fool i confess
i am in winter of my years but somehow i have blossomed

Lynne Savitt studied with Diane Wakoski in the early seventies and subsequently taught writing workshops at various colleges, community centers, and prisons. Her first poem was published in *Playgirl* magazine in 1974. Over the years her poems have appeared in dozens of literary magazines, including *13th Moon, Second Coming, Home Planet News*, and *Poetry Now*. She has been a featured poet online from *Desolation Angels* and *Rusty Truck*. She was the recipient of the Madeline Sadin Poetry Award from *The New York Quarterly*. She co-founded and edited *Gravida* and co-edited *Caprice* and was also a contributing editor to *Redstart* and *StonyHills*. Savitt has twelve published poetry collections. Her latest book is *Too Late for Valentine's Day*, 2012. Born in Brooklyn, New York in 1947, she is a single parent of two children and grandmother of seven. She resides on eastern Long Island.

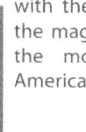
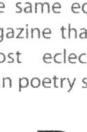
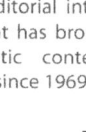
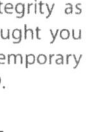

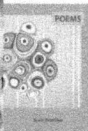